IOWA
UNDERGROUND

A GUIDE TO THE STATE'S
SUBTERRANEAN TREASURES

GREG A. BRICK

trails books

AN IMPRINT OF BOWER HOUSE

DENVER

Iowa Underground: A Guide to the State's Subterranean Treasures. Copyright ©2004 by Greg A. Brick. All rights reserved. Printed in Canada. No part of this book may be used or reproduced in any manner whatsoever without written permission except in the case of brief quotations embodied in critical articles and reviews. Bower House books may be purchased with bulk discounts for educational, business, or sales promotional use. For information, contact Bower House P.O. Box 7459 Denver, CO 80207 or visit BowerHouseBooks.com.

Editor: Stan Stoga
Project Manager: Mike Martin
Assistant Project Manager: Erika Reise
Photos: Greg Brick and Cindy Doty
Designer: Todd Garrett
Cover Designer: Margaret McCullough

Library of Congress Control Number: 2004104308
ISBN: 978-1-931599-39-9

10 9 8 7 6 5 4 3 2

Disclaimer: Risk is always a factor in backcountry and cave travel. Many of the activities described in this book can be dangerous, especially when weather is adverse or unpredictable, and when unforeseen events or conditions create a hazardous situation. The author has done his best to provide the reader with accurate information about backcountry travel as of the writing of this book, as well as to point out some of its potential hazards. It is the responsibility of the users of this guide to learn the necessary skills for safe travel, and to exercise caution in potentially hazardous areas, especially on steep and difficult terrain. The author and publisher disclaim any liability for injury or other damage caused by backcountry traveling, or performing any other activity described in this book.

Who does not remember the interest with which
when young he looked at shelving rocks, or any
approach to a cave?

—*Thoreau, Walden*

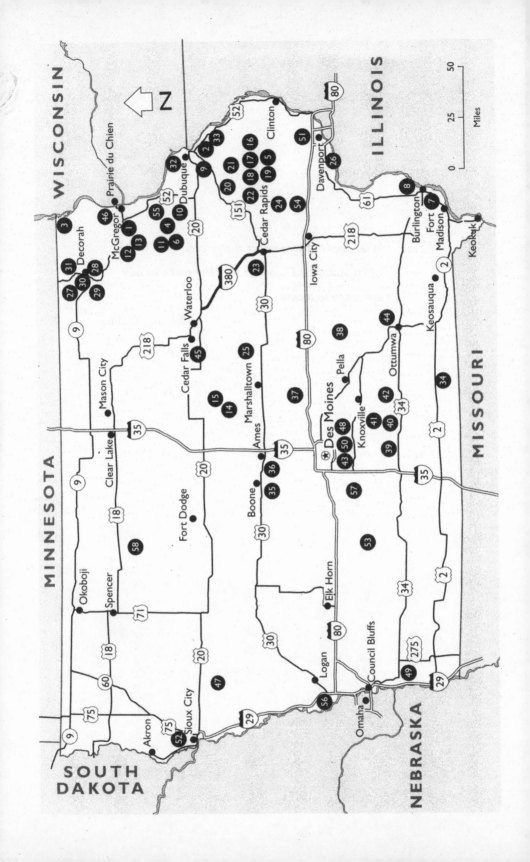

Contents

Section II
Mining Museums

Section IV

Other Sites ....

Appendix

Introduction

IN 1673, THE FRENCH explorers Father Jacques Marquette and Louis Joliet, canoeing down the Wisconsin River to where it met the Mississippi, became the first white men to see the area that would later become Iowa. Looking up at the towering river bluffs, Marquette wrote in his journal that the area seemed like "a large chain of very high mountains"—conjuring up almost Himalayan imagery. Like the story of the blindfolded men describing an elephant, it depends which end you grasp first. Had Marquette and Joliet spent more time exploring the area west of the Mississippi, they would certainly have gotten an entirely different impression of its terrain.

Even if they had more closely observed the landscape, they would never have imagined that it abounds in subterranean attractions—all told, more than a thousand of them. And over three hundred years later, most people today, even those who think they know Iowa, likewise would never suspect as much. For example, in my extensive research for this book, I spoke with many people who had been caving longer than myself and who were surprised to learn that there was a subterranean attraction just down the road that they had never heard about. And some Iowa natives might not know that the main cave area of Iowa—"Little Switzerland," as it was dubbed long ago in reference to its rugged, scenic landscape—is in the quadrant of the state east of Interstate 35 and north of Interstate 80. Samuel Calvin, the state's pioneering geologist, described northeastern Iowa as "a land of gorges," bristling with "castles and towers and flying buttresses." One of the purposes of this book is to show that this cropland- and prairie-dominated state contains a wonderful array of underground treasures that can be enjoyed by novice and experienced cavers alike.

Another surprise: mining, too, is well represented in Iowa. It's no accident that lead mining features prominently on the Iowa state seal, on which lead pigs and a lead smelter are depicted. In the late eighteenth century, Julien Dubuque, the first white settler in what is now

Iowa, was a lead miner who profited handsomely from his efforts. Also, remnants of the coal-mining industry are found throughout the southern half of the state, but you have to know what you're looking for to recognize them. Apart from the big two—lead and coal—many other rocks and minerals have been mined in the state. They include gold panned from glacial stream deposits at many locations around the state; iron ore dug from Iron Hill near Waukon; silica mined at Clayton, creating an immense labyrinth of passages; limestone quarries and mines at Stone City—the heart of Grant Wood country; and the gypsum beds at Fort Dodge, from which the Cardiff Giant, the legendary hoax, was carved to thrill a nation in the years following the Civil War.

With all of Iowa's underground attractions, there is a crying need for an up-to-date guidebook that details the wonders that they offer. A previous publication, The Caves of Iowa, was compiled by Iowa caving organizations largely in the 1950s and 1960s—before the discovery of Coldwater Cave, Iowa's largest, and before many of the areas described in this book were even opened to the public. Few copies of the earlier book were distributed, and it is now extremely rare. It is a learned but daunting tome, the entries heavy with the boring "grapes and crane flies" notations beloved of the old-fashioned cave indexer. Relying on this book, the would-be cave explorer, bent double with gear, is frequently directed to a site using ephemeral, long-vanished landmarks, like the forking of a deer trail.

That's not to say there hasn't been tremendous progress in documenting Iowa's caves and mines in the years since. The local chapter of the National Speleological Society, called the Iowa Grotto, continually discovers and surveys new caves. It maintains the Iowa Cave File, which, with one cave per page, is now about six inches thick. But these records are not available to the general public. So, for years there has been a need for a guidebook to publicly accessible caves and mining sites in Iowa.

This book is an attempt to fulfill that need. It contains something for everyone, from neophytes to seasoned explorers new to Iowa. Section I, "Caves," is the heart of the book, describing show caves and wild caves. For example, Spook Cave near McGregor, with its underground boat tours, is a perennial favorite among Iowa show caves. The densest concentration of wild caves open to the general public, on the other hand, is found at Maquoketa Caves State Park, where you can either spend a whole day getting down and dirty or merely stroll along a lighted causeway through the largest of the caves. Section II covers mines, concentrating on lead and coal. The Dubuque area, with its Mines of Spain Recreation Area, is full of lead history, and many of the county museums in southern Iowa have constructed actual coal mine replicas that you can walk through. Section III, "Living Underground," deals with all aspects of subterranean life, from the lowliest bugs to the quasi-troglodytic lodge dwellers of western Iowa. Section IV, "Other Sites," is a smorgasbord of subterranean attractions, from the banal to the bizarre. Here you can find brewery cellars in a state with strong prohibitionist tendencies (Guttenberg), subterranean steamboats (the Bertrand), the greatest religious grotto in the Midwest (West Bend), and even a trip to the center of the Earth (Bridgewater). The two appendices, with suggestions for additional caving opportunities and lists of useful written resources and Web sites, are intended for those who would like to explore more of this wonderful state on their own.

The reasons for visiting and exploring underground sites are as varied as the people who explore them. Some are intrigued by the mystery of the underground and its darkness, while others are eager to dispel the shadows with the aid of a bright light and a surveyor's field book. Some are sport cavers, while others are scientifically motivated. Some take up cave photography as a rewarding hobby. For educators, field trips to caves can teach proper stewardship of the land. For others, exploring the underground can be an interesting new way to study the state's geology and history. Families that pay a visit to a "show cave" for the first time might fall in love with the experience and vow to see others. But whatever their interests, this book will be the best starting point for anyone who wants to enrich his or her underground experiences.

What to Wear and What Gear to Take

This section applies mostly to the exploration of wild caves, but it may come in handy when poking around other geological sites as well. Most of the caves featured in this guide are reasonably safe and require no special clothing other than a jacket and full-lenth pants—and a willingness to get dirty. I wear a jacket even when I don't need one to stay warm because it protects the skin from the abrasiveness of cave surfaces. Some cavers prefer coveralls, but others feel as if they are tied up in a gunnysack when wearing them.

For those caves requiring "full caving gear," however, something more is required. At a minimum, you should always carry at least three different sources of light, which should be tested beforehand. I have gone on trips where several lights have failed in succession, and I was glad to have the backups. It is best to have a hard hat with a mounted light too because it frees up a second hand for moving through the cave. Once, in a stream cave in West Virginia, I was using a hand-held light and stepped over an underwater drop-off. I tried to swim—with one hand! I always wore a mounted light after that.

A hard hat, apart from serving as a mount for your light, protects your head from falling stones, and a chin strap ensures that the hat won't go flying off at a critical moment. Gloves, knee pads, and hiking boots complete the outfit. For wet cave passages, boots and chest waders should also be considered. Over the years, however, I have found that even the best-quality waders will soon shred in cave passages, so instead I merely allow my clothes to get wet, making sure to bring dry clothes to put on before the drive home. I save the delicate, pricey waders for situations where I'll be in deep, cold water for an extended time.

Other things that I carry in my cave pack include a compass (it works just as well underground as it does above) and a length of rope to use as a safety line when navigating steep slopes or in similar tricky situations. And for the determined cave prospector, bug dope is a must!

Bring food and water, even if only for the hike to and from the cave. I have found that certain foods, such as sandwiches, seem to take on the taste of the cave after a while, so I prefer candy bars (for energy), granola bars, and trail mix or the like.

Avoid caving alone—even in small caves. It doesn't seem like a big deal to hike out to a remote cave and, while inside, step over a few boulders or crawl through a few pinches, but if you sustain even a comparatively minor injury, like a sprained ankle, that same distance will seem far greater on the way out.

Keep in mind that the appearance of a cave may change with the seasons. Thus, a cave that I describe as containing deep water may be bone dry during a drought year, or vice versa. Also note that even parks that claim to be open year round will sometimes have a walk-in policy only during the winter season, so there may be cold-weather hiking involved. And just to play it safe, wear blaze orange during hunting season, especially in designated wildlife areas.

Finally, a word about ethics and conservation. Iowa, compared with many states, has a liberal and inviting policy with regard to cavers, and it would behoove all who venture into its caves to preserve this privilege. Respect landowners' wishes, and do not trespass. Do not damage caves, remove things, or leave trash. Damage to cave formations takes ages to heal. A commonly quoted statistic is that it takes one hundred years to form a cubic inch of calcite, a process analogous to adding a new coat of paint to the formation every hundred years. While the growth rates of cave formations vary greatly, what is certain is that they grow very slowly.

If you would like to get into caving more seriously after reading this book, I urge you to consider joining the Iowa Grotto, which can provide specialized training. Founded in 1949, this cave club holds monthly meetings at Trowbridge Hall on the University of Iowa Campus in Iowa City and for many years has published a sterling newsletter, *The Intercom*, which has won awards. Their address is— Iowa Grotto, Box 228, Iowa City, IA 52244.

Oh yes, one more thing: You might want to drop those fond words "spelunker" and "spelunking" from your vocabulary, as they carry pejorative connotations among cavers themselves. You're a caver now!

In preparing this book, I have personally visited all of the sites described—and many others—logging almost 10,000 miles in one year amid a busy teaching schedule. In the process, I have accumulated two sky-kissing stacks of letter trays full of notes. In a guidebook that attempts to cast a wide net, I have had to occasionally depend on information supplied by others, which I have double-checked whenever possible. Some of this information is contained in the "List of Resources" (p. 211). On the other hand, I have made an effort to incorporate new, previously unpublished information in every entry. I have taken pains to correct some errors in the resource literature and hope that I contribute as few as possible of my own. I hope that this book helps people enjoy the underground wonders that Iowa has to offer. ▪

Acknowledgments

I WOULD ESPECIALLY like to thank: John Park, mining historian and owner of Stone Rose Publications, for reviewing the manuscript, Paul Rasmussen, owner of Spook Cave, for opening his cave in the off-season, and Doris Green, who founded this series of underground guidebooks.

Among the many other people who rendered assistance with this book, I would like to thank Rick Allensworth, Mills County Conservation Board; Justin Armstrong, tour guide, Life Engineering Foundation; Jennie Bailey, Iowa Museum Association; Don Brazelton, Iowa Association of County Conservation Boards; Phil Broder, environmental education coordinator, Starr's Cave Nature Center; Martin Burke, Madrid Historical Society; Dr. Kenneth Christiansen, Grinnell College; Beverly Cross, director, Jasper County Historical Museum; Kathryn Dixson, John L. Lewis Mining and Labor Museum; Kevin Drees, Blank Park Zoo; Bertha Finn, Anamosa historian; Shirley Frederickson, Golden Hills Resource Conservation and Development; Maureen Harding, curator, Herbert Hoover Museum; Cathy Henry, Driftless Area National Wildlife Refuge; Bill Heusinkveld, Appanoose County Historical Museum; Sally Hinz, director of special projects, Putnam Museum; Mary Howes, Iowa Geological Survey Bureau; Charles Irwin, executive director, Boone County Historical Society; Dennis Laughlin, director, Battle Hill Museum of Natural History; Pete Malmberg, historic and cultural resources coordinator, Dallas County Conservation Board; Bonnie McDonald, Brick School House Museum; Milly Morris-Amos, Ottumwa historian; Dean Nelson, Camp Wyoming; John Pearson, Iowa Department of Natural Resources; Jean Cutler Prior, Iowa Geological Survey Bureau; Duane Rieken, Hardin County Conservation Board; Naser and Patricia Shahrivar, Old Brewery Art Gallery; Gary Siegwarth, Big Springs Trout Hatchery; Ted Smith, Glenwood American Indian Earth Lodge Society; Gary Soule, show caves historian; Mike Stegmann, Marshall County Conservation Board; Dean Stocker, Monroe County Historical Museum; Deacon Gerald Streit, director, Grotto of the Redemption; Mike Whye, travel writer, and Greg Wolf, Clinton County Conservation Board. ■

Section I
Caves

ONE EARLY IOWA cave explorer waxed poetic about "the great pillared halls of the underground empire of Iowa." While this assessment might seem rather exaggerated, there is little doubt that Iowa boasts an impressive array of caves—many of which can be easily explored. Of the 50,000 known caves in the United States, Iowa boasts more than one thousand, ranging from tiny, womblike voids all the way to Coldwater Cave, the state's largest, with more than 16 miles of surveyed passages. And even though the number of Iowa caves is dwarfed by that of neighboring Missouri—which has more than 6,000 caves—Iowa's public parks contain more caves than any of its other neighbors. That's good news for cavers of all skill levels.

What's more, responsible explorers are actually welcome in Iowa's parks. My native state, Minnesota, has nothing remotely comparable to Maquoketa Caves State Park, for example, where visitors are actually invited to explore more than a dozen wild caves. The architects of Iowa's parks have something to be proud of when it comes to underground exploration. And the privilege should not be abused!

Most of Iowa's caves are found in its **karst** landscape, which is marked by underground drainage—in contrast with the more familiar landscapes sculpted by surface streams. On karst terrain, disappearing streams enter sinkholes, flow through caves, and reemerge as springs. Many place-names in karst areas contain the word devil, an indication that early settlers tended to regard such landscape features as out of the ordinary.

Iowa's best-developed karst, where most of its caves are found, is located in the northeastern corner of the state—long ago dubbed "Little Switzerland" for its rugged features. This area, along with portions of adjacent states, has also been called the **Driftless Area** because it is supposedly devoid of drift, or glacial debris. But in 1976, in recognition that drift is, in fact, present in the Driftless Area, this part of Iowa was renamed the **Paleozoic Plateau** because the bedrock here was laid down during the Paleozoic Era (600 to 230 million years ago). Yet, while the rocks themselves are thus very old, the caves in them are much younger—usually less than a million years.

The term **cave** has been defined in various ways, but it usually includes the sense of an underground space large enough for a human being to fit into. The related term **rockshelter** refers to shallow caves or cliff overhangs.

There are several different kinds of caves in Iowa and several ways in which they can be classified. What follows is a highly simplified account. **Solution caves**, formed in carbonate bedrock, such as limestone or dolomite (a magnesium-rich limestone), are the most abundant kind found in the state. Carbonic acid, the ubiquitous natural acid, forms when carbon dioxide, produced by the respiration of organisms in the soil, dissolves in groundwater. The acid eats out caves along preexisting vertical joints and horizontal bedding planes in the underlying bedrock. Many caves initially developed under **phreatic** (water-filled) conditions. Later, when the water table dropped—due to the successively deeper erosion of nearby valleys by surface streams—the cave passages drained, entering a **vadose** (air-filled) phase. **Speleothems** (cave formations) such as **dripstone** (**stalactites** and **stalagmites**) and **flowstone** were deposited during this stage. **Soda straws** are the hollow, tubular precursors of the typically carrot-shaped stalactites, while **helictites** resemble thin, twisted stalactites. **Grapes** and **popcorn** are varieties of **coralloids**, a nodular mineral deposit that forms on cave walls and ceilings. A cave that has abundant speleothems is said to be "well decorated." Solution caves can be roughly divided into **branchwork caves**, which contain branching passages, **network caves**, with fairly straight passages formed along intersecting joints, and **maze caves**.

The two great cave layers of Iowa are the **Galena Limestone** and the **Hopkinton Dolomite**. Or, they could be called the "Lead-Bearing Layer" and the "Swiss-Cheese Layer," respectively. The Galena layer, laid down during the Ordovician Period (500–425 million years ago), contains Iowa's lead deposits as well as its largest caves. The Hopkinton, above the Galena, was laid down subsequently, during the Silurian Period (425–405 million years ago). Both rock layers were originally deposited as lime sediments in the warm, shallow seas that covered Iowa long ago. The Hopkinton usually formed maze caves under artesian conditions, whereas the Galena caves tended to follow long, straight joints in the rock. The Hopkinton rock, especially, is riddled with little Swiss-cheese-like holes, called **vugs**, which cavers often refer to as "solutional sponging."

Iowa's Silurian rocks are most prominently exposed in the **Niagara Escarpment**—so called because geologists have equated it with the rocks exposed at Niagara Falls. The Niagara Escarpment is an ancient, buried reef that loops around the Great Lakes, passing diagonally through northeastern Iowa, where it typically manifests itself as a wooded slope. The Mississippi River deflects eastward where it impinges against this resistant escarpment, forming the "nose" that juts from Iowa's eastern border. Some of Iowa's oldest and best-loved parks and preserves are located along the Niagara Escarpment—one of the reasons being that not much else can be done with such scenic, rugged land!

Other geologic layers in Iowa also contain caves, of course. Rocks of the Cambrian Period (600–500 million years ago), the first period of the Paleozoic Era, host Black Hawk Cave in the northeastern corner of the state. Mosquito Cave, in Cedar Rapids, was formed in Devonian-age limestone (405–345 million years ago). Caves in the southeastern corner of the state, around Burlington, are found in limestone laid down during the Mississippian Period (345–310 million years ago). In Kentucky, rocks of Mississippian age host the longest cave system in the world, Mammoth Cave—more than 350 miles long and still counting!

Pseudokarst caves, as the name would suggest, mimic real karst, but no solutional process is involved in their formation. Some geologists use the term pseudokarst rather loosely—basically, any nonsolutional void—while others have given it a restricted meaning. There are several kinds. **Mechanical caves** are created by earth movements, as when rocks separate along joints or faults, sliding along an underlying shale layer, leaving narrow gaps, of which the Decorah Ice Cave is a good example. **Rock cities**, with their charming, leaf-carpeted "streets" and "avenues," are also formed by this mechanism—as at Brush Creek Canyon and White Pine Hollow. **Talus** (boulder) **caves** are formed by the spaces between boulders. While not an important category in Iowa—a small talus cave is featured in the entry on Echo Valley Park—some New England talus caves are thousands of feet long and have actually been developed as "show caves", for which an entrance fee is charged. **Piping caves** were created by flowing groundwater washing away individual grains of rock. The reddish Pennsylvanian (310–280 million years ago) sandstone underlying so much of Iowa provides examples, such as Wildcat Cave, near Eldora.

Many of these cave types can be found at Maquoketa Caves State Park (described later in this section), which forms a sort of microcosm of the Iowa cave world. ▪

Show Caves

SHOW CAVES are natural caves that provide accommodations for visitors and, more often than not, require an entrance fee. While the terms show cave and commercial cave are often used interchangeably, some cavers interpret the word commercial broadly, including any economic use, such as mushroom growing or the mining of guano, onyx, and saltpeter. On the other hand, there are show caves in parks which, since they are government run, are not technically "commercial."

Show caves are what most Americans think of when they consider a visit to an underground attraction. The earliest documented show cave in the United States is Grand Caverns in Virginia, which was regularly frequented by visitors as early as 1809. The earliest-known show caves in the Upper Midwest are Fountain Cave in Saint Paul, Minnesota, which was in operation in the 1850s, and Chute's Cave in Minneapolis, which gave torchlight boat tours in the 1870s.

At present, Iowa has two operating show caves, **Crystal Lake Cave** (commercialized in 1932) and **Spook Cave** (commercialized in 1955). However, at least five other Iowa show caves have been open to the public in the past. The earliest was **Timmen's Cave**, located in Union Park, Dubuque. A 1909 postcard depicts tourists on an electrically lighted stairway inside the cave. Indeed, Union Park was initially developed by a trolley company to showcase the use of electricity, but it never really recovered from a devastating flood in 1919, and the cave was blasted shut.

The 1930s were the golden decade of show caves in Iowa. **Decorah Ice Cave** was commercialized by Stanley Scarvie in 1929 and operated until 1941. Scarvie strung lights in the cave and built a zoo nearby. He also operated **Glenwood Cave**, nine miles east of Decorah, from 1931 to 1935. It featured a 1,200-foot tour by boat—foreshadowing the boat tours at Spook Cave. In later years, under the moniker "Kegger Cave," Glenwood became notorious as a major party spot for local college students. In 1936, Scarvie opened **Wonder Cave**, just outside Decorah, which remained in operation until 1976. The cave featured a Petrified Forest, a floodlit Rock of Ages, and the "World's Largest

Known Stalactite" (in fact, it was nothing of the sort). In 1937, Gerald Mielke, who would later develop nearby Spook Cave, opened **Wompi Cave**, billed as "Iowa's Deepest," to the public, but it closed during World War II when he could no longer obtain gasoline for the electrical generator that powered the lights. The cave contained a bizarre formation resembling an elephant's head.

The biggest prize for commercialization never materialized, however. In 1974, a report was presented to Iowa Governor Robert Ray, recommending commercialization of the recently discovered Coldwater Cave, the largest cave in the state. An enormous expense would have been involved, so the suggestion was tabled. ■

1

Spook Cave
Clayton County

SPOOK CAVE began with a mysterious spring at the base of a 90-foot bluff along Bloody Run Creek, near McGregor. Strange sounds emanating from a small opening at the spring resulted in the name Spook Hole. Gerald Mielke, a local resident who had experience developing show caves in the Upper Midwest, saw commercial possibilities. In 1953, he blasted into the bluff and discovered a sizable cave—along with flowing water inside the cave that was causing the spooky sounds. He blasted open a separate work entrance in a side ravine and built a ramp down into the cave. He spent the next two years removing tons of rock and mud. The cave opened for business in 1955 and remains the only underground boat tour in Iowa.

The ticket stand and gift shop for your cave tour is Spook Cave Lodge, created by grafting two local schoolhouses together. It contains a wall of historic photos documenting the commercial development of Spook Cave. The tour departs from the dock in one of Mielke's original seven custom-built aluminum boats, with a quarter-horsepower electric trolling motor at the bow. The boat floats across a millpond, under a footbridge, and into the cave entrance. The milldam maintains a sufficient water depth to float boats in the cave stream, known as Spook River. In winter, the millpond is drained away, and Spook River falls to its natural, shin-high depth. Mielke built the nearby Old Mill for the purpose of generating electricity for the cave lights, but the waterwheel didn't produce much power, so the mill became merely ornamental. The millpond flows into Bloody Run Creek, which empties into the Mississippi River at Marquette. The creek got its name because this area was a favorite hunting ground for soldiers from Fort Crawford, across the Mississippi in Prairie du Chien, Wisconsin. They washed animal hides in the creek.

Spook Cave developed in the Galena limestone, and the tour guides will tell you that it is 750,000 years old. Spook River flows on top of the underlying, impervious, Decorah shale. The cave is an elliptical rock tube with domes at intervals. The cave drains water over 13 square miles of land surface, discharging 1.75 million gallons per day. The water becomes turbid after a heavy rainfall or during spring snowmelt, carrying agricultural sediments into the cave from the land

The Spook River, haunted with ghostly reflections, pours from the mouth of Spook Cave, near McGregor.

surface above and depositing them in the boat channel. As a result, the cave needs to be dredged each winter in the off-season.

The roof of the cave is very low in places, requiring you to lean forward, almost to the point of placing your head in your lap. The first such place, just inside the entrance, is called Lover's Lane for this very reason—you may need to get cozy with the fellow occupants of your boat! The handles affixed to the cave walls aid navigation in the tight spots, but they are for the use of the guide only. Hands should be kept inside the boat because they could easily get crushed when the boats bang against the walls. Deep grooves are worn into the rock from the constant rubbing of the boats.

As your boat passes from the artificial, blasted section into the natural cave proper, a side passage, called Mielke's Crawl, comes into view on the right side. The roof suddenly lifts, and you float into the Big Room, the largest room in the cave, 30 feet high and 110 feet long. Look for the trapdoor in the ceiling, the location of the former upper entrance to the cave. Although it was originally thought that tours could be brought in this way, the opening created a strong air current that began drying out the cave formations, so it was sealed. The left wall of the Big Room, made up of jumbled rock and mud, is called the Landslide.

Upstream from the Big Room, on the right side, is the zebra-striped Flowstone Wall. The white stripes of pure calcite alternate with black stripes containing manganese compounds. On the ceiling here you will see the bottom of a sinkhole. While it's dry most of the time, this hole showers water after a heavy rainfall. On the left, you pass the illuminated Wishing Well, which is ornamented with formations that broke off during commercial development of the cave.

After rounding the S-bend of Spook Cave, the tour guide is sure to tell the story of Old Joe for comic relief. Old Joe was a solo cave explorer who didn't return one day, so they say, and his boat was found capsized in Spook River. Scratch marks were found on the chocolate-colored mud banks where he tried to save himself—in a foot or two of water, at best—a feat that is roughly equivalent to drowning in a bathtub. His body was never found, but the guide will point out his surprisingly new hat resting on the mud bank. You may purchase a similar hat in the gift shop!

You now enter another low-ceilinged, elliptical rock tube. About midway through, as you approach the Dog Tooth Formations, you again have to hunker down in the boat. This cluster of toothlike stalactites, which includes a "hairy" stalactite, is protected by a screen on the ceiling. Just after that, the Frozen Waterfall will give you a chance to tip your head back in the other direction as you peer up into the 35-foot-high dome. The Frozen Waterfall, an undulating, flowstone-covered wall, was the high point of the original cave tours in the 1950s and the place where boats turned around to head back for the entrance. It wasn't until years later that the next segment, Formation Alley, was opened for business. Formation Alley has a well-developed "lifeline" (as guides are fond of calling joints in the roof of the cave) crammed with stalactites and ribbed with "bacon strips"—a kind of cave formation that resembles thin strips of bacon. During a winter trip into Spook Cave, kindly arranged by the owner, Paul Rasmussen, I found this to be a lifeline in a different sense: it harbored numerous moisture-loving eastern pipistrelle bats.

Near the end of the tour you enter the Dome Room, 40 feet high and 120 feet below the surface. Illuminated by your guide's flashlight, the Rock of Ages, a waterproof enamel painting on glass depicting a woman clasping a stone cross in a surging tide, is balanced on a high rock ledge in the cave. The passage is wide, leaving ample room for the boats to turn around. Just beyond is Half Mile Bar, spanning the passage like a chin-up bar. Despite its name, it's only about a quarter of a mile from the entrance. Beyond the bar, there is a dam across the stream designed to stop agricultural sediments from filling in the boat channels, which they seem to do anyway.

Beyond the dam, which marks the end of the commercial tour, the passage is filled with huge rock slabs and ends at the Sump Room, which contains the deepest water in the cave. Cave divers have explored a thousand feet beyond this sump through water-filled passages.

On the grounds outside Spook Cave, just downstream from the boat entrance, you'll see a spring called **Beulah Fails** pouring from the cliff. This little spring cave will give you some idea of what the original Spook Hole may well have looked like. Beulah was a small railroad town located where the campground is today. The town was swept way in a flood many years ago.

Directions: Located west of McGregor. From U.S. Highway 18, turn north on Spook Cave Road, follow the signs.

Season/hours: Open daily, 9:00 a.m. to 6:00 p.m., Memorial Day to Labor Day; weekends, 9:00 a.m. to 4:00 p.m., May 1 to Memorial Day and Labor Day to October 31. Last cave tour leaves one half hour before closing. Fee.

Length: The boat tour, through 1,000 feet of passage, lasts 40 minutes.

Precautions: The cave is "Always 47 Degrees," according to the brochure, so wear a sweater or jacket.

Amenities: "93 Acres of Fun," including gift shop, game room, cabin rental, campground, playground, picnicking, hiking, swimming, trout stream.

Contact: Spook Cave and Campground, 13299 Spook Cave Road, McGregor, IA 52157.
Phone: (563) 873-2144.

Crystal Lake Cave
Dubuque County

BEFORE THE discovery of Coldwater Cave in 1967, Crystal Lake Cave was the largest known cave in Iowa, and it remains the state's largest show cave today. James Rice discovered the cave in 1868 while digging for lead. He sunk a 40-foot shaft into a hillside south of Dubuque and struck a cave passage. The cave proved barren of ore, however. It was called Rice's Cave at first, and then, as became the trend, took the name of subsequent owners, becoming Linden's Cave. It wasn't commercialized until 1932 when Bernard Markus, one of the original miners, christened it Crystal Lake Cave and built the pretty, white, latticework cage around the façade of the entrance building that you see today. Formerly obscure, Crystal Lake Cave came to the attention of the scientific world in 1938 when geologist J Harlen Bretz, from the University of Chicago, published a classic scientific study of caves in the Galena Formation.

The commercialization of Crystal Lake Cave was a Herculean task. Many of the original cave passages were barely large enough for a raccoon to squeeze through, let alone a human being. Observe, for example, the prominent rock ledge at head and shoulder level along much of the present tour route; this marks the level of the original stalagmitic floor of the cave! This floor was broken up and removed, after which several feet of underlying clay were excavated, leaving comfortable passages about six feet high and two feet wide. A few low points along the route, like Tall Man's Misery, still remain, however.

The tour begins at the bottom of the concrete stairway, where you find yourself in a long, straight passage heading east into the hill. Very soon you discover the pattern: the main passages are oriented east-west and are linked together by shorter, north-south passages. This is a network cave.

The first of the many cave formations you will encounter is Saint Peter's Dome, a stump-shaped stalagmite, followed by the Honeycomb Pillars. A thermometer on the wall here registers 50 degrees Fahrenheit, the cave's year-round temperature. At the eastern end of this straight passage is the namesake Crystal Lake, full of green coins. This narrow body of water is said to be 28 feet long, 3 to 4 feet wide, and 2.5 feet deep.

The tour crosses over to an even longer parallel passage. Walking farther into the hill, you pass the Ostrich, an interesting composition of fallen stalactites that have fused together at odd angles. The Cliff Dwellers, a cluster of stalagmites perched on a flowstone shelf, marks a jog in the passage. Swiss Cottage Roof is a mass of flowstone that resembles the sod roofs of houses in the Swiss Alps. On the opposite side of the passage is Lot's Wife, an unusually pure white stalagmite that resembles a pillar of salt.

The passage continues beyond the jog as Coral Avenue, so named because of the rare anthodites—flowerlike clusters of white crystals that sprout from the ceiling in a part of the passage called Hanging Gardens. Farther along is Cathedral Dome, containing the Chandelier (a prominent cluster of stalactites) and the Little Frozen Niagara, a flowstone deposit. Finally, at the easternmost and deepest point of the tour, one hundred feet underground, you reach the Lop-Eared Dog. Below it is a little brown jug, bearing the date 1880, supposedly left behind by miners. As you look back to where you came from, you can still see Lot's Wife, 180 feet away—a very long, straight shot!

Looping back through a parallel passage you encounter the Goose Hangs High—a stalactite with a bulbous extremity, like a goose swinging from a hook. In addition to the goose-headed stalactites, other strange forms seen in Crystal Lake Cave are barbed stalactites, and stalagmites that resemble an upthrust arm with an open hand at

Crystal Lake Cave, south of Dubuque, has an impressive variety of formations— many of them with fanciful names.

the top, imitating a gesture of baroque statuary. Helictites, whose twisting shape is controlled by capillary forces, sprout from the walls in many places.

Stroll through Character Lane, a sort of museum of formations that were (unavoidably) broken during commercialization of the cave. Strangely shaped pieces of the original floor ended up here. See, for example, the Turtle, a large, carapacelike chunk of the floor, or Noah's Ark, a boatlike chunk, complete with tiny stalagmitic figures on deck, ready for any deluge. Pass the Cliff Dwellers again and continue on to the King's Throne. The Lost Gardens, often depicted on postcards of Crystal Lake Cave, will be found here. The end of the passage, illuminated in rosy light, contains a display of lead mining tools.

The tour turns south and passes under the Liberty Bell. The Chapel, a flowstone-coated dome illuminated with green light, occupies a side joint. Weddings have been held here, and it's the highest room in the cave, with 16 feet of relief. Next comes the Petrified Forest, a group of soda-straw stalactites protected by chicken wire.

Entering the final parallel passage, you head west toward the exit. Along the way, you'll see the Glacier—an icelike mass of flowstone—followed by the Fairy Castle and the Pipe Organ.

Crystal Lake Cave has far more attractions than are described here. Indeed, it contains the highest percentage of named and labeled features that I've seen in any show cave. And the tour route covers only a small portion of the total length of the cave. There is an additional 1.5 miles of unexcavated passages. The most noteworthy feature in the undeveloped area is the Flat Room, which is far larger than any room on the commercial tour: 90 feet long, 30 feet wide, and 7 feet high. Crystal Lake's well-decorated sister cave, **Kemmling Cave**, is private.

Directions: Five miles south of Dubuque on U.S. Highway 52, follow the signs.

Season/hours: Open in May on weekends 9:00 a.m. to 5:00 p.m. Open daily from Memorial Day to Labor Day from 9:00 a.m. to 6:00 p.m. Fee.

Length: The tour covers three-quarters of a mile and lasts 45 minutes.

Precautions: Sweater or jacket recommended. There are steep stairways at the beginning and end of the tour.

Amenities: Souvenir shop, snack bar, picnic grounds.

Contact: Crystal Lake Cave, 7699 Crystal Lake Cave Drive, Dubuque, IA 52003. Phone: (563) 556-6451. Web site: www.crystallakecave.com

Erratics

An erratic is a stone transported from its parent source to another spot by a glacier or its streams. Erratics were sometimes called "foundlings"—transported, then abandoned, by glaciers. Some early geologists mistakenly attributed erratics to distant volcanic eruptions!

Erratics can be used to track the path a glacier has traveled. A 67-pound nugget of native copper, for example, is thought to have traveled 500 miles from the Lake Superior area; it's now on display at the University of Iowa. Native Americans regarded erratics as spirit stones or medicine rocks, and myths and legends grew around them. The most intriguing myth is that they possessed the power of locomotion—an uncanny foreshadowing of modern glacial theory. Some were painted with red ocher, which represented blood—a symbol of life. Tobacco offerings were often left at the base of these stones. In 1920, an image found on an erratic near the town of Fertile, Iowa, was said to be the footprint of a prehistoric Eskimo, carried south by the glaciers! The "footprint" was probably only a petroglyph, or rock carving.

Iowa, especially the northern part, is studded with erratics, most of them hard rock types, such as granite, which is why erratics were sought out for use as millstones. Erratics are especially conspicuous on the prairie, where they served as "pilot rocks" for guiding the pioneers. The largest erratic in Iowa, located near Nashua, was originally 50 feet across. A cluster of nine erratics, collectively called Rock City, crowns a hill near Sumner. Erratics also marked the boundary of the Black Hawk Purchase. Boulder Church, in Waterloo, was built with stone quarried from a large erratic. The Civilian Conservation Corps used erratics to build rustic lodges in state parks. Erratics also became gravestones. White Cross Rock in Dubuque, for example, bears intersecting veins of white quartz, forming a natural cross. The Stone Man, near Fayette, is a granite boulder bearing an uncanny resemblance to a human head and torso. Most erratics, however, were cleared away when fields were prepared for planting crops and were stacked up into stone walls.

My favorite erratic—from a subterranean perspective—is Ormston Rock, located on a farm near Waverly. It contains a shallow cave that shelters livestock on hot summer days.

Wild Caves

W ILD CAVES constitute the vast majority of natural caves—
those that are not show caves. The wild caves discussed in
this section are natural caves that are either located on
public land or on private land where there is public access of some
sort. In addition, two natural-looking caves, Bixby and Eldora, which
are likely of human origin, are featured.

There are so many wild caves on public land in Iowa that I won't
pretend to include every last one of them. Many are obscure—even to
knowledgeable people. For example, I have found and explored significant caves in Iowa parks in which the person in charge asserted
that none existed; I was just acting on a hunch, based on the geology
of the area, when I went ahead anyway and looked for them.

Accordingly, this section of the book presents the best, most
instructive examples of wild caves in the state, rather than a complete
listing. Providing descriptions of all known caves would have produced an unwieldy and less useful section. The countless Hopkinton
dolomite caves, for example, all begin to look alike after you've visited
a few of them. Iowa cavers have even been challenged to come up with
names for them, resorting to awkward, three-word cave names in
recent years. It's rather like trying to come up with unique names for
the individual holes in a piece of Swiss cheese.

Black Hawk's Cave
Allamakee County

SOUTH OF New Albin—the northeasternmost town in Iowa—is Black Hawk Point, a rock pinnacle riddled with voids situated in a wildlife area of the same name. The rocky outcrops soar more than three hundred feet above the mouth of the Upper Iowa River. Here you will find **Black Hawk's Cave** (sometimes called Gabbett's Cave), which has a long and romantic history.

In 1832, the United States acquired the area comprising the eastern third of Iowa for 14 cents an acre—a coercive land deal that became known as the Black Hawk Purchase. The so-called purchase was actually punishment for Chief Black Hawk and his allies having begun the Black Hawk War earlier that year. The problem went back to 1804, when land in Illinois, Missouri, and Wisconsin was too easily ceded to the United States by certain members of the Sac and Fox tribes, perhaps under the influence of liquor. Chief Black Hawk hotly disputed the validity of this cession.

In 1831, squatters had the temerity to invade the site of the chief's very own village near Rock Island, Illinois. He yielded reluctantly and withdrew to the Iowa side of the Mississippi River. But the following year he went back across the river to harvest the crops his tribe had planted the previous season and the Black Hawk War was on. The young Abraham Lincoln served in this conflict and famously described it as a "chicken-stealing expedition." The chief was defeated at the Battle of Bad Axe in Wisconsin—a detail that some historians dispute.

According to the plaque at Black Hawk Point, "it was claimed by some that Chief Black Hawk was captured here in 1832, not across the river in Wisconsin as other authorities agreed." Tradition states that the chief hid in a cave on Black Hawk Point for several days. The pinnacle would indeed make a superb observation post and signal point. The plaque adds that "Sac and Sioux Indians fought at the base of Black Hawk Bluff during the Battle of Bad Axe which ended the Black Hawk War in 1832." In any case, the chief was eventually removed to Jefferson Barracks, near St. Louis, Missouri, while the infamous "deal" was negotiated.

Looking skyward at the high promontory from the gravel turnout on State Highway 26, you may feel intimidated by a trek to Black Hawk's Cave. But don't despair; the climb is not that bad, although it's certainly fatiguing. You're not going to the top, after all—merely to the area containing caves around the base of the bluff. In any case, it's not advisable to visit the caves located higher on the sheer faces of the cliff—leave those for the eagles!

The entrance to Black Hawk's Cave is shaped like a gaping mouth, with an opening 17 feet wide, 4 feet high, and 7 feet deep. A hawk petroglyph is carved above the entrance. The image's deep, sharply incised lines clearly indicate that it was carved with a steel tool, however, so it's not a genuine, prehistoric petroglyph. The view of the valley below, through the gnarled cedars, is spectacular. The nearby cliff juts out like the beak of a hawk, and it's hard to tell whether this feature is natural or contrived.

No lights are required in the dry, sandy interior of the cave. The renowned Iowa archeologist Ellison Orr (1857–1951) excavated Black Hawk's Cave and found pottery, charcoal, clam shells, and bear bones. Animal hides may have been draped over the entrance of the rockshelter for additional protection from the elements. He published his findings in a classic paper on the rockshelters of Allamakee County in 1931. He concluded that the prehistoric human inhabitants of the cave were bear-eaters. Orr was also involved in the establishment of the nearby **Effigy Mounds National Monument**.

There are more than one hundred other rockshelters in northeastern Iowa. Many of them, like Black Hawk's Cave, were formed by natural weathering of the Cambrian-age Jordan sandstone, while others are found in the overlying Oneota dolomite. Good locations to see additional rockshelters are the wildlife management areas (WMAs) along State Highway 26, particularly Lansing WMA and Yellow River State Forest WMA. At the latter, **Paint Rockshelter** has a long history. A narrow shelf can be seen about 40 feet above the base of the bluff. Native Americans, using mineral pigments mixed with fat, created pictographs here; most have long since eroded away.

There is another cave with a similar name, **Black Hawk Spring and Cave**, located in Burlington. See the description later in this section.

Directions:	Black Hawk Point Wildlife Area is two miles south of New Albin at the intersection of State Highway 26 and Black Hawk Road.
Season/hours:	Daily, 4:00 a.m. to 10:30 p.m. Free.
Length:	7 feet.
Precautions:	The hike uphill to the cave is strenuous. Don't attempt caves on the shear cliff face. Wear blaze orange during hunting season.

Amenities: Parking lot, information kiosk, flowing well, hiking.

Contact: IDNR, Upper Iowa Unit, 903 Commerce Drive, Suite #4, Decorah, IA 52101. Phone: (563) 382-4895.

Bixby Ice Cave
Clayton County

B IXBY ICE CAVE, the scene of an old lead-mining operation in Hopkinton dolomite, resembles a Halloween fog machine at times. The fog rolls down the mossy stone stairway from the cave gate, a scene worthy of the entrance to Count Dracula's castle. The fog well illustrates how cold air travels down slopes. The air creates a microenvironment where unusual plants can grow, including dwarf scouring rush, ground pine, muskroot, northern currant, and rare lichens.

The cave gate at **Bixby State Park and Preserve** is permanently locked, but visitors are invited to come up and look through the bars. As one gets closer to the gate on a hot summer day, the cool breeze feels pleasant, but after a while it begins to seem painfully cold. Especially noteworthy are the steel beams and jacks holding up the great mossy boulder that forms the roof of the entrance room, with the roots dangling down behind it. The passage heads down into a jumble of boulders, for a total length of 30 feet. Pieces of rotten wood, the remains of an earlier door to the cave, litter the slope. A small lake sometimes fills the back end of the cave. The cold blast of air comes not from the back end of the cave—as one might expect—but from a ceiling crevice midway through the cave. On the floor below this downdraft, ice can be seen between the stones, even in the hottest part of summer.

After checking out the ice cave, head for **Cool Cave**, which is located by walking north along the gravel road uphill to the first rock outcrop on the left side. There are several holes but only one that's large enough to enter. Here, there is also a cool blast of air, but no fog pours from this cave. The passage is 40 feet long and 1 to 2 feet wide.

Cold air pours from Bixby Ice Cave on a hot summer day, supporting a community of rare plants.

Due to the crevice in the floor, the cave is not recommended for children. Reportedly, the cave contains gypsum, suggesting that it is very dry.

In 1854, when the Bixby farm occupied this land, the owner let the public use it free of charge, and it eventually became a state park. Also visit nearby **Mossy Glen State Preserve**, three miles northwest of Bixby. The glen contains sinkholes, springs, waterfalls, and Mossy Glen Cave—a nasty little crawlway full of spiders that is not recommended for the novice. Another scenic gem in the vicinity is **Fountain Springs Park**, three miles northeast of Greeley in neighboring Delaware County. The springs here were used to power a mill for grinding wheat in the days before Iowa became a major corn-producing state.

Directions: From State Highway 3 in Edgewood, follow the signs two miles to the preserve: head north on North Franklin Street, which turns into a gravel road at the north edge of town and becomes Fortune Avenue. Follow it down into the glen, drive across the ford over Bear Creek, and park at the pavilion on the right side. From the parking lot, follow the path up Bear Creek and cross on the stepping stones. Keep to the right wall of the valley, and you will soon see the cave.

Season/hours: Daily, 4:00 a.m. to 10:30 p.m. Free.

Length: 30 feet

Precautions: Cool Cave is not recommended for children owing to the crevice in the floor.

Amenities: Hiking, picnicking.

Contact: IDNR, Backbone State Park, 1347 129th Street, Dundee, IA 52038. Phone: (563) 924-2527. Web site: www.state.ia.us/parks

Skull Cave
Clinton County

I N SHERMAN PARK, on the scenic Wapsipinicon River, a giant skull glares out at you from behind the trees. Undaunted, you bravely crawl into the skull's gaping jaws and, after diverting yourself a while in its pitted brain cavity, crawl back out through one of the eye sockets. They don't call this Skull Cave for nothing!

After entering the cave on your hands and knees, you emerge into a sit-up room. The cave floor can be wet and muddy during certain seasons, so gloves are appropriate. If you visit during the summer, the brush around the cave entrance is often alive with hungry mosquitoes, but you can find refuge from them in the cool, far recesses of the cave, which has about 50 feet of passage. The cave curves around a corner to the right, so you soon find yourself in total darkness if you venture far enough into the "cranium." The walls of the cave have a spongelike appearance, pitted as they are by countless little pockets, called vugs, typical of the Hopkinton dolomite. The vugs contain mud, indicating

After crawling in through its "mouth," the author exits from the "eye socket" of Skull Cave. Photo by Cindy Doty.

that the cave has been flooded in the past by the Wapsipinicon River. About 10 feet into the cave, however, watch for the connection to the upper level, which is otherwise easy to miss. You can stand up completely at this point and climb up into the cave's eye sockets.

Very close to Skull Cave are two smaller caves within 20 feet of each other. At the time of my visit, mud blocked the entrance of the cave immediately to the south, but the rooms were still visible. The southernmost of the three is a horseshoe-shaped cave, the effect created by a pillar at the entrance; the interior is 3 feet high and there is 30 feet of passage.

To get to the caves, head toward the campground in Sherman Park. After passing the observatory (a little white dome on your right) follow the gravel road as it descends onto the floodplain of the Wapsipinicon River and then forks. The left fork parallels a dolomite outcrop and ends at a picnic table at the southernmost tip of the park. The big, old silver maple next to the fork marks the location of Skull Cave.

Sherman Park, located on the north bank of the Wapsipinicon River in Clinton County, is contiguous with the **Wapsi River Environmental Education Center**, on the south bank in Scott County. They share more than a mile of river between them, providing 432 acres of land for 13 threatened or endangered species.

Directions: From Exit 284 on Interstate 80 (the location of the Iowa 80 Truck Stop—billed as "The World's Largest"), go north on County Road Y40 (60th Avenue) to the town of Dixon, then west on County Road Y4E (Davenport Street, which becomes Big Rock Road) to 52nd Avenue. Head north on 52nd Avenue to 310th Street. Go east on 310th Street to 57th Avenue, and go 1.5 miles north. You will cross over the Wapsipinicon River, and the park entrance is just beyond, on the left side.

Season/hours: While the park is open year round, the caves may be flooded and inaccessible during high water in the spring. Free.

Length: Various.

Precautions: Jacket, gloves, and lights.

Amenities: Picnic tables, playground, campground.

Contact: Clinton County Conservation Board, P.O. Box 68, Grand Mound, IA 52751. Phone: (563) 847-7202. Web site: www.clintoncountyiowa.com

Backbone Cave
Delaware County

BACKBONE CAVE is deservedly one of the most popular attractions in Backbone State Park. From the parking lot near **Balanced Rock**, in the northern part of the park, follow the trail through the woods to the bluff, where a stone stairway leads up to the cave.

Backbone Cave is a low (4 feet) and wide (10 feet) passage in Hopkinton dolomite. The cave consists of a single passage that jogs between two parallel joints, for a total length of 210 feet, and there's no chance of getting lost. The cave has an undulating mud floor, and the walls have a spongelike appearance created by countless little pockets. Upon entering the cave, follow the passage to the left and then left again, where there is a large breakdown block. Stooping through a low space you will encounter the polished stump of a stalagmite, nine inches in diameter, like the stump of a petrified tree. Just beyond, you can stand up again. Here you will find an hourglass-shaped column, two feet high, and a flowstone covered wall. For me, this was the most enjoyable part of the cave.

From this point on, however, the passage dwindles in size. After hunkering down and making your way through the dark, rocky tube—occasionally pausing to rest your knuckles on the red mud floor—your own backbone may be ready to give out. A short side passage to the left leads to a tiny flowstone room that can be entered only by crawling sideways through a narrow aperture, which is not for everyone. The main passage eventually becomes a belly crawl. You then come to a stalagmitic shelf—a remnant of a former cave floor. Just past that, to your right, there is a small cavity where, if you listen long enough, you may be able to hear a strange, periodic sputtering noise. It's rather like listening to the sea in a seashell. Time to make your way back to the entrance!

Back on the outside, you may want to visit nearby **Richmond Springs**, one of the larger springs in Iowa. The springs rise within two low, rock-walled basins near the head of Fenchel Creek, a trout stream that runs through the park. According to the informative plaque, the spring emerging from the "Niagara limestone" (an obsolete name for

This stone stairway leads to Backbone Cave, a popular attraction in Iowa's oldest state park.

the Hopkinton) has an output of 2,000 gallons per minute and a constant temperature of 48 degrees Fahrenheit. The spring water used to be piped to a trout hatchery in the park.

Returning to your car, drive south through the park toward the **Devil's Backbone**—the namesake feature of the park. Along the way, the road dips into the Maquoketa River valley, where there was once a path (now abandoned) called the Catacombs Trail that wound among crevasses in the rock. The park road winds back uphill to the Backbone, where there is another parking lot. Park here and have a look at the Backbone itself, where there are a few more small caves.

The Backbone is a high ridge of dolomite, one-quarter of a mile long, in a bend of the Maquoketa River. The hike along the crest of the Backbone, which is clothed with xeric (dry) vegetation, is very scenic. A deep crevice known as the **Devil's Stairway** rives the Backbone from top to bottom. Only rock climbers should attempt this diabolical descent, however. On the east face of the Backbone (which is to your left as you walk along) you will see a man-made stone stairway leading down to the **Devil's Oven**, a cave that honeycombs a separate rock pinnacle. It's easy to climb up into this cave, where there is room enough for several people to sit and enjoy a view of the Maquoketa River valley. The shadowed path that follows the foot of the Backbone here is known as Lover's Lane.

Dedicated in 1920, Backbone was Iowa's first state park. Other park attractions include the Civilian Conservation Corps Museum, which is open on summer weekends, and the oldest known tree in Iowa, a cedar more than six hundred years old. The park has been called "an island of flora" because many of the plants found here are uncommon in the surrounding croplands. Backbone Lake, created by damming the Maquoketa River, occupies the south end of the park. Here, there are rustic cabins available for rental.

Directions:	Four miles south of Strawberry Point on State Highway 410.
Season/hours:	Daily, 4:00 a.m. to 10:30 p.m. Free.
Length:	210 feet.
Precautions:	Jacket, gloves, and lights.
Amenities:	Picnic tables, campground, year-round cabins, fishing.
Contact:	Backbone State Park, 1347 129th Street, Dundee, IA 52038. Phone: (563) 924-2527. Web site: www.state.ia.us/parks

7

Black Hawk Spring and Cave
Des Moines County

THE RESIDENTS of Burlington were startled one morning in 1989 to learn that one of their favorite little lakes, Lake Starker, in **Crapo Park** (pronounced "cray-po"), had suddenly vanished. In its place was a gaping sinkhole. To be sure, the lake had been leaking for a decade prior to its disappearance, but no one had given it much thought. The mystery was solved when someone figured out that the lake had drained into a beautiful old cave spring on the nearby river bluffs.

A century earlier in the 1880s, what is now Black Hawk Spring was known as Indian Springs and was a popular picnic spot. An oval, bronze plaque installed above the cave entrance in 1914 by the Daughters of the American Revolution reads, "Black Hawk Spring, Named in honor of the famous warrior Chief Black Hawk who with his tribe used this spring when camping in this vicinity."

A square masonry pillar at the mouth of Black Hawk Cave supports the 20-foot-wide entrance. The stream of springwater issuing from the cave divides and goes around the pillar. If you look closely you may be able to see scuds in the water. Scuds—technically known as "amphipods"—are freshwater shrimp, a fraction of an inch long. They "scud" along on their sides and are generally a sign of good water. Upon leaving the cave, the stream tumbles over a black, mossy waterfall and down through a pretty little glen where there are lime-green shales. At the bottom, the stream enters a culvert, passes under railroad tracks, and wanders among the willows briefly, before joining the Father of Waters.

Exploring the cave will involve walking through cold stream water, so boots are advisable. The entrance room of the cave, beyond the pillar, has been enlarged by frost action. The opening funnels down to a narrow passage just high enough for the average person to walk through. The bedrock here is Mississippian-age Burlington limestone, and it's crammed with "Cheerios" fossils—pieces of sea-lily stems. After wading through shin-deep water for a hundred feet, you will come to a small waterfall at waist height. From here on, the cave

The double-barreled entrance to Black Hawk Spring and Cave, nestled among the rocky ledges of Burlington, is adorned with an oval DAR historical plaque.

becomes a rock tube one to two feet in diameter, containing the cold stream. Do not go past this point! Shining your light ahead through the foggy tube, you can see the passage veering off to the right, and beyond that it curves back again to the left and becomes too small to follow. A wetsuit and training would be required to explore beyond this point.

There are several rockshelters in the park. Follow the **Black Hawk Trail**, formerly known as Lover's Lane, along the base of the limestone outcrop, and you will see some of them.

Crapo Park was a gift of local philanthropist Philip M. Crapo in the 1890s. The hundred-acre park is best known for its arboretum, which contains every tree indigenous to the region, and for its bluff-top river scenery, with a nice view of Illinois across the Mississippi

River. In 1805, the first American flag to fly over what is now Iowa was hoisted in this area by Lieutenant Zebulon Pike, for whom Pikes Peak State Park, near McGregor, is named.

Directions: Crapo Park is located on Main Street, south of downtown Burlington, along the Mississippi River. Park at the Hawkeye Log Cabin Museum, follow the fenced footpath down into the wooded ravine south of the cabin, you will soon hear and see the spring.

Season/hours: Daily, 5:00 a.m. to 11:00 p.m. Free.

Length: Total length of the cave is 146 feet, but only the entrance is easily traversable.

Precautions: Jacket, gloves, and lights. Wear boots or expect to get your feet wet. Do not enter the stream crawlway!

Amenities: Arboretum, Hawkeye Cabin Museum, picnic tables.

Contact: Burlington Parks and Recreation Department, City Hall, 400 Washington Street, Burlington, IA 52601. Phone: (319) 753-8117. Web site: www.burlington.lib.ia.us/city/localgo/parks/guidepar.htm

Starr's Cave State Preserve
Des Moines County

THE FLINT CREEK VALLEY, which bisects Starr's Cave State Preserve, has been called the Grand Canyon of Des Moines County because of its towering limestone bluffs. The flint contained in the limestone was so prized by Native Americans for making arrowheads that the nearby city of Burlington was once known as Flint Hills.

Before venturing into the preserve's caves, a visit to the Starr's Cave Nature Center is a must for anyone who wants to gain a deeper appreciation for the area's rich geologic features. It occupies the big red barn—which, in days gone by, was also once the Sycamore Inn, a nightclub! The center's excellent exhibit, "The Geology of Starr's Cave," features a geologic column and hand specimen from every rock unit that outcrops in the preserve. You learn, for example, that the Burlington Formation—the resistant limestone that forms the prominent, overhanging cliffs in the park—contains over one hundred species of fossils. Southeastern Iowa is especially well known for its crinoids—the Cheerios-like fossils that are pieces of the stems of extinct, flowerlike animals, also known as sea lilies. Crinoids formed extensive submarine meadows in the Iowa seas of long ago. Charles Wachsmuth (1829–96), a Burlington merchant who hunted for fossils among the ravines and ledges of that city, wrote a monograph that made the area world famous for crinoids.

After touring the nature center's other exhibits—including the artificial beaver lodge—visit nearby **Small Cave**, reportedly an old zinc prospect. To get there, head north on the trail leading away from the parking lot, a nice woodland walk along the banks of Flint Creek. At the end of the trail, a quarter mile later, a slope leads up to the cave. The circular cave, 20 feet in diameter, is of standing height, with lime-green lichens encrusting the walls. Abundant crinoid fossils can be seen in the roof. The rock joints running through the ceiling are several inches wide and filled with a red, claylike soil that is slowly making its way down from above.

Another cave, **Devil's Kitchen**, is located in the bluffs directly across Flint Creek. You can either wade across or, depending on the water level, hopscotch across the dark, flinty gravel bars without get-

The stairway to Starr's Cave is far easier than climbing a tree trunk, as visitors once had to do!

ting your feet seriously wet. You can also return to your car, temporarily exit the preserve, and drive a half mile farther north along Irish Ridge Road to an overlook perched two hundred feet above the creek. Follow the long, steep woodland trail from the overlook downward. Near the bottom, the trail drops into a ravine, and, where the ravine meets Flint Creek, you will find the cave on the left side. Devil's Kitchen is similar to Small Cave, except that it's about 30 feet in diameter and has two entrances, providing plenty of light.

A bit farther along the same trail, which follows the banks of Flint Creek, you will come to the stairway leading to **Starr's Cave**. An interpretive plaque next to the stairway tells the story of the cave. You learn that among the bat species inhabiting the preserve are big and little brown bats, red bats, gray bats, and the federally protected Indiana bat. That's why the cave has a gate that's locked in winter—with openings just large enough for the bats to fly through!

Reportedly, Starr's Cave served as a hideout for a gang of horse thieves in the 1850s. Before the Civil War, the cave may also have served as a hiding place for runaway slaves on the Underground Railroad (see the sidebar "Iowa's Underground Railroad" on page 184). William Starr settled here in the early 1860s, and the ruins of the old farm buildings can be seen along the **Rossiter Heritage Trail**. In 1877, local boys supposedly discovered a trapdoor into the back end of the cave, leading to large rooms containing relics of the thieves. However, no such back entrance or large rooms were found during the mapping of the cave. The area was popular with picnickers in the early days, and the cave appears on old postcards. Before the stairway was built, explorers could reach the cave entrance only by shimmying up a tree trunk propped against the bluff!

At the top of the stairs, 30 feet above the streambed, the strong, vertical rock joint along which the cave developed is especially noticeable in the cave floor. The Gothic or spade-shaped cave passage, formed in limestone filled with crinoids, follows a set of joints trending northeast. Generally speaking, the cave passage, 300 feet long, gets smaller the farther in you go—while the formations get larger! There are no side passages, so you can't possibly get lost.

The first hundred feet is the easy part—a straight walking passage. But soon the passage hunkers down to a dry, dusty, hands-and-knees crawl. If you plan to continue into this part of the cave, you must wear gloves and kneepads or the sharp, flinty gravel will cut your skin to shreds, as I learned the hard way. Eventually, you will come to a small room containing flowstone, where you can sit and take a breather. From here the passage angles left, and you can belly crawl 20 feet into a 12-foot-high dome, called the Autograph Room, containing even more flowstone. Stand up and stretch. But don't even think of entering the damp, red mud crawlway that leads off from this dome! In 1976 an experienced Iowa caver was trapped in a tight S bend in this terminal crawlway for six hours until rescued by a fireman. Instead, make your way back to the entrance, and just hope you don't meet the next visitor coming along the narrow way, as one of you will have to retreat!

Directions: From U.S. Highway 61 north of Burlington, turn east on Sunnyside Avenue to Irish Ridge Road (County Road X60). Turn north on Irish Ridge Road and go half a mile to the main park entrance on the left. The overlook parking lot is a half mile farther north on Irish Ridge Road.

Season/hours: Open daily, 6:00 a.m. to 10:30 p.m. The Nature Center is open Monday through Friday, 9:00 a.m. to 3:00 p.m., Sundays 1:00 to 4:00 p.m. Starr's Cave itself is locked between October 1 and April 1 for bat hibernation season, and at this time the Nature Center is also closed. The two small caves are open year round. Free.

Length: Starr's Cave is 300 feet long.

Precautions: Starr's Cave requires jacket, gloves, kneepads, and lights. Elbow pads would also be nice. The two small caves don't require equipment.

Amenities: Nature Center, picnic tables, hiking.

Contact: Des Moines County Conservation Department, Starr's Cave Nature Center, 11627 Starr's Cave Road, Burlington, IA 52601.
Phone: (319) 753-5808.
Web site: www.state.ia.us/parks

Catfish Cave
Dubuque County

JULIEN DUBUQUE, the famous lead miner for whom the city of Dubuque was named, lived at the mouth of Catfish Creek two hundred years ago. Perhaps, while relaxing on a summer evening with his Meskwaki Indian friends, he sat in this very cave on the banks of the creek.

Catfish Creek State Preserve occupies the northern half of the **Mines of Spain Recreation Area** (see section II, "Mining Museums," for a description of the abundant mining-related features in this preserve). Catfish Cave is a smoke-blackened hole located at the base of a 170-foot, cedar-crowned bluff of Galena dolomite—on top of which is the Julien Dubuque Monument.

South of Dubuque, drive to the preserve's parking lot, located at the north side of the bridge over Catfish Creek. Near the base of the

Julien Dubuque may once have used this cave, located on the banks of Catfish Creek below the monument that bears his name.

stairs leading up to the monument, turn and follow the gravel trail out to the little boat dock on the creek. Continue beyond the dock, following a dirt path heading downstream along the north bank of the creek. A railroad trestle, bridging the mouth of the creek, will come into view. The trail ends at a rock outcrop, and you should walk along the banks of the creek and maybe even get your feet wet, rather than scramble along the outcrops and risk slipping. Within a hundred feet or so you will find a smoke-blackened hole in the bluff, about 10 feet above river level.

Catfish Cave is a splendid place to see how caves develop along lines of weakness in the rocks—in this case, a master joint that runs all the way to the top of the bluff. The cave is 12 feet high, 20 feet deep (measured from the dripline of the bluff), and 15 feet wide. Frost action has enlarged the cavity. A thick band of chert—a flintlike rock—runs through the wall. It's obvious, from the fire pit and beer cans, that the cave is well known locally.

There are other rockshelters along Catfish Creek and elsewhere in the preserve, some of which show evidence of prehistoric habitation dating as far back as 8,000 years ago, the Archaic Period.

Directions: From U.S. Highway 52 on the south side of Dubuque, take the Grandview Avenue exit, turn east at the top of the ramp, and follow the signs for the Julien Dubuque Monument. Turn right (south) just before the monument and drive downhill to where the road crosses Catfish Creek. Park at the bridge. Or enter from the south by way of the Mines of Spain Recreation Area.

Season/hours: Daily, 4:00 a.m. to 10:30 p.m. Free.

Length: 20 feet.

Precautions: The trail leading to Catfish Cave requires scrambling up a rock outcrop.

Amenities: Hiking, picnicking.

Contact: E. B. Lyons Interpretive Center, 8999 Bellevue Heights, Dubuque, IA 52003. Phone: (563) 556-0620. Web site: www.state.ia.us/parks

White Pine Hollow State Preserve
Dubuque County

S AMUEL CALVIN, a well-known early Iowa geologist, writing in 1900 about the area that would later become White Pine Hollow State Preserve, said, "The outcrops of the Niagara [dolomite] in the beautiful gorge of Hollow creek, in the northwest corner of Liberty township, give rise to many picturesque castles and towers and flying buttresses which afford keen delight to all visitors who are capable of being impressed with natural grandeur." Luckily for succeeding generations, the wilderness value of the area was recognized by many others interested in its preservation. The Dubuque High School Nature Club built a cabin here in 1932 and used it for nature study. White Pine Hollow was designated a state forest in 1934, a state preserve in 1968, and a National Natural Landmark in 1972.

White Pine Hollow, so called because of the rare groves of white pine, is Iowa's best boreal forest relic—its cold, damp conditions providing habitat for plants, such as Canada yew, more commonly found in southern Canada. Covering more than one square mile, the preserve contains over 625 species of plants and is especially rich in mosses, prompting one of its devotees to declare, "There is more moss here per square inch than any place I know." The growing season here is about three weeks shorter than

A block of dolomite leans sideways at Castle Rocks in White Pine Hollow State Preserve.

Vertical Caving in Iowa

Vertical caving involves ascending and descending shafts and pits inside caves. In the early days of caving, this was often done using a bosun's chair—similar to the seat of a swing set—originally used to rescue people at sea. However, the chair required a powerful motor at the top to hoist the explorer. Rope ladders, something also borrowed from marine practice, subsequently came into vogue. But it wasn't until the 1960s that the single-rope technique (SRT) revolution, led by Bill Cuddington of Virginia, really took hold in the United States. Without SRT, which freed cavers from bulky climbing gear, the deepest caves of the world would probably remain unexplored even today.

Midwestern cavers sometimes have the reputation of being merely "horizontal" cavers. After all, there are few really deep caves in the Midwest. However, although most of Iowa is fairly flat, some of its underground passages are much different. Exploration of the abandoned lead mines under the city of Dubuque, for example, required vertical techniques because the mines are usually accessible only through deep shafts. Iowa cavers not only wholeheartedly adopted vertical techniques, but improved on them, developing new climbing devices, such as the Iowa Safety Rack, for descents and the Iowa Cam, the first practical mechanical ascender.

Vertical caves also led to the first known caving fatalities in Iowa history. On February 28, 1987, seven cavers from Grinnell College set out to explore Miller Cave near Postville. After descending the 108-foot drop into the cave and having a look around, the cavers began to exit. In the meantime, it had started to rain. Water began pouring into the otherwise dry pit. One caver became trapped in the ice-cold waterfall while ascending his rope and rapidly succumbed to hypothermia. The person who went to his rescue, ascending another rope, drowned in the attempt. The remaining cavers stayed at the bottom in a passage that protected them from the waterfall until help arrived. Sandbags were used to divert the stream at the top, and the remaining cavers were lifted to safety.

anywhere else in Dubuque County.

White Pine Hollow is also known for its geological features, of course. There are 320 feet of vertical relief within the rugged preserve—from the spring-fed creek to the soaring bluffs. The so-called Hogback—a ridge or backbone of dolomite isolated by a bend of Pine Hollow Creek—is especially interesting. At the southern tip of the Hogback is a small "rock city"—known locally as **Castle Rocks**—formed by blocks of dolomite that have slid downhill, leaving large gaps between them. In the deep, shaded recesses of this mossy metropolis, bats can be observed flying about, even in daylight!

A little higher up the slope, and parallel to the bluff line, you will find a line of sinkholes, formed where part of the bluff has separated from the remainder by several feet—but not enough to form isolated blocks. Most of these sinkholes are mere dimples filled with leaves, but others are open sinkholes leading to extensive crevice caves. The caves are stable and have plenty of hand- and footholds, and they can be followed down quite a distance. A good example is found on the Hogback, in the immediate vicinity of Castle Rocks.

The largest cave in White Pine Hollow, **Yew Ridge Cave**, is over seven hundred feet long and should only be attempted by trained cave explorers. The caves in this preserve have been the focus of considerable bat research. Six species of bats exist here, including the federally protected Indiana bat.

Directions: This preserve has two entrances: east and south. The best way to get to the cave area is to use the east entrance because it leads to a gravel access road that allows you to drive into the heart of the preserve; however, it also requires a vehicle with high ground clearance and should not be used in wet weather because it fords Pine Creek at two points. From Luxemburg, take U.S. Highway 52 north for 1.5 miles to Lake Road. Turn west and go three-quarters of a mile to Heim Road. Keep to the right onto Heim Road and continue one-half mile until you see the sign on the left side of the road. Enter the preserve and drive about one-half mile to where the road ends, at a small gravel lot near the top of a ridge. Hike the trail due west until reaching the bluff overlooking Hollow Creek, and then follow the edge of the bluff south to the Hogback. For the south entrance, take State Highway 3 west for two miles to White Pine Road; turn north, the road ends at the boundary of the preserve. Park, and hike the trail leading north.

Season/hours: Daily, 4:00 a.m. to 10:30 p.m. Free.

Length: Various.

Precautions: Hard hat, jacket, gloves, and lights. The caves should not be attempted unless you are physically fit; they are not appropriate for children. The caves can be difficult to locate; be prepared for strenuous hiking over rough terrain and few trails; allow a full day. Carry a compass for orientation in the woods.

Amenities: Hiking.

Contact: IDNR, Yellow River Forest, 729 State Forest Road, Harpers Ferry, IA 52146. Phone: (563) 586-2254. Web site: www.state.ia.us/parks

11

Brush Creek Canyon
State Preserve
Fayette County

BRUSH CREEK CANYON STATE PRESERVE contains Iowa's best example of a "rock city." Rock cities, as geologists call them, are found at many places in the United States. They form where giant blocks of rock, called "float" or slump blocks, separate from the parent cliff just enough to leave intersecting "streets" and "avenues" in the spaces between. In certain parts of the country they are also informally called "bear towns," but you needn't worry about meeting bruin here. At Brush Creek the passages are one to three feet wide, and the cliffs are nearly one hundred feet high. Children will love threading the mazes!

This preserve, like several others discussed in this book, is located along the Niagara Escarpment. Huge blocks of Hopkinton dolomite have rotated and slid downhill on the underlying Maquoketa Shale. Some of them have slid all the way downhill into the stream. Others are topped with small prairie remnants. Upon first visiting Brush Creek Canyon I was reminded of Rock City Park, near Olean in upstate New York, where the "city" is composed of a very different rock type, and you have to pay to get in—while this one is free!

This preserve, on land once part of "Allen's Wildwood Springs," does not have a well-developed trail system, so you'll have to find your own way along the faint deer trails through 217 acres of woods. From the parking lot, head north (downstream) along Brush Creek for one-half mile. Stay high on the slope, near the rock outcrops, until you see another stream, Moine Creek, coming in from the west. Here, along the ridge separating Brush Creek and Moine Creek, you will find the rock city. You will see several openings but keep going until you find one that doesn't require gymnastics to get to.

As an example, I will describe one of the routes that I took during my own visit. Entering the rock city by one of the entrances on the Brush Creek side, I walked steeply uphill through a leaf-carpeted avenue about two feet wide. Enough light filtered down from above that a flashlight wasn't really necessary. After some distance I came to an intersection and turned to the right. This new avenue curved somewhat and I came to a place where I could easily climb up-wards.

After navigating a stoop-way where the walls pinched together at the top, forming a true cave, I emerged through an opening into the Moine valley, just as the sun was setting. I had passed completely through the ridge! Entering the city again by way of another, Gothic-shaped entrance on the Moine Creek side, I took a different route back to the other side. There's actually no chance of getting lost inside.

If you go past Moine Creek and continue downstream along Brush Creek—which eventually joins the Volga River—you will pass a perfectly round rock tube in the bluff above you, accessible only to rock climbers. Up the next side valley, at the northern tip of the preserve, is **Blue Spring**—a deep, circular pool, 20 feet in diameter. The spring rises among a jumble of float blocks, and does indeed appear bluish in color. Since the spring is on private land just outside the boundaries of the preserve, permission must be obtained before getting up close.

This is one of several entrances to the intersecting "streets" of the rock city in Brush Creek Canyon State Preserve.

Directions: From State Highway 187 in Arlington, head north on Diagonal Road, which turns into E Avenue, which dead-ends at the preserve, two miles north of town.

Season/hours: Daily, 4:00 a.m. to 10:30 p.m. Free.

Length: The rock city has hundreds of feet of passages.

Precautions: Jacket, gloves, and lights. Allow two to four hours and plan to get back to your vehicle before sundown to avoid losing your way in the woods. The hike is over rugged slopes.

Amenities: Picnic tables and pavilion, restrooms.

Contact: Volga River Recreation Area, 10225 Ivy Road, Fayette, IA 52142. Phone: (563) 425-4161. Web site: www.state.ia.us/parks

12

Dutton's Cave
Fayette County

WHILE HUNTING for bees and killing rattlesnakes one day
in 1848, Lorenzo Dutton found a cave. Along with Falling
Springs, located on the opposite side of the town of West
Union, it soon became a favorite spot for local picnickers. Reportedly,
the cave contained a lake on which people could row boats. Today,
standing among the jumble of dry boulders, it's hard to imagine such
a scene.

The broad, smiling mouth of Dutton's Cave, as it came to be
known, is located in a county park of the same name, at the foot of an
impressive 80-foot cliff that is part of a box canyon in the Niagara
Escarpment, an ancient reef. Boulders, covered with lime-green
lichens, sit in the mouth of the cave like rotten teeth. On either side of
the cave, springs gush forth water, joining to form a stream that runs
noisily down the canyon. However, there is no water flowing from the
mouth of the cave itself—at least not during dry weather. High on the
beetling brow of the cliff is a waterfall notch, also usually dry. A
stairway to the right of the cave entrance leads to the top of the bluff,
over the lip of the waterfall, and to the upper campground in the park.

Dutton's Cave, a single passage in the Silurian-age Edgewood limestone, is 6 feet high, 20 feet wide, and 80 feet long. Bird's nests are
tucked among ledges in the ceiling at the entrance. The sound of dripping water becomes louder as you make your way among the boulders
and continue deeper into the cave. In winter, these drips form massive
icicles. In other places, smooth, rounded pockets indent the ceiling—
remnants of the embryonic conduits from which the cave originally
developed. Plant debris, washed in through sinkholes on the uplands
beyond the cave, suggests the force of water that roars through the
cave during wet weather.

At the right inner corner of the cave is Steeple Cavern, an oval shaft
30 feet high and 6 feet in diameter that narrows toward the top. Here,
you find yourself in complete darkness and feel a cool downdraft
from the "steeple." The walls of the shaft glisten in a beam of light.

At the left inner corner of Dutton's Cave, among the boulders, is
the entrance to the Lower Passage, more than three hundred feet long.
Do not enter this passage! The low, wet crawlway, with its abundance

The gaping mouth of Dutton's Cave is located at the head of a box canyon in the Niagara Escarpment.

of raccoon footprints, leads to deep, cold water and requires a wetsuit. During wet weather, water completely fills this tube and spills out into the upper level, eventually draining from the mouth of the cave. Indeed, the two-hundred-foot-long gorge leading up to the cave was formed by the collapse and retreat of the cave's roof as the spring gnawed its way into the bluff.

Directions:	From U.S. Highway 18, two miles east of West Union, watch for signs. Go north one mile on Ironwood Road (gravel) to 250th Street, head right, toward Picnic Area, for a quarter mile, pass sign for Dutton's Cave, go downhill, and park. Follow the footpath over the wooden bridge, turn right at the pavilion, and follow the stream. Where the mowed field ends and the brush begins, you will see a sign, "Caution: Trail Slippery When Wet." Continue walking another 200 feet up the gorge.
Season/hours:	Open all year. Park closed to noncampers after 10:30 p.m. Free.
Length:	The upper, dry level of the cave is 80 feet long.
Precautions:	Jacket, gloves, and lights. Do not enter the lower, water-filled passage. The water is cold, requires a wetsuit, and the passage floods during wet weather!
Amenities:	Picnic tables, playground, campground.
Contact:	Fayette County Conservation Board, 18673 Lane Road, Fayette, IA 52142. Phone: (563) 422-5146 or -3613.

13

Talus (Boulder) Cave
Fayette County

HIKING THROUGH **Echo Valley State Park** is like going on safari. You encounter inexplicable stone foundations in the jungle of underbrush. Standing sphinxlike, they seem like the remains of a lost civilization. At twilight, with mist rolling through the valley, the park has a haunting quality. Best of all, there are caves!

Driving through the hundred-acre park, located near West Union, can be disorienting because of all the crazy twists and turns in the road. Beyond the entrance, after passing a picnic area in a scenic amphitheater of high bluffs, cross the Otter Creek ford and head up to the stone pavilion on top of the hill, where you will see a sign that reads "Past Echoes." It states, "From this site in 1936 a beautiful man-made lake could be seen, which was created when a dam was built by the Civilian Conservation Corps." Peering down into the dense tangle of brush nowadays, it's difficult to imagine that a lake ever existed down there. That's because, within 10 years of its construction, the lake, held back by a pyramid-shaped dam, filled up with silt from surrounding farm fields. Without a lake, the park lost much of its appeal to the locals. After a long period of neglect, Echo Valley State Park was reborn in the 1980s, at which time some interesting historical finds were made. Workers discovered a tunnel apparently used as a millrace and even a long-abandoned picnic area hidden in the dense brush!

Park at the pavilion and walk back to the deep railroad cut that you passed while driving up the hill. After hiking through the cut a quarter mile, you will come to massive stone bridge abutments with the date 1890 clearly visible. The Rock Island Railroad once bisected the park, but the rails were later removed as part of the Rails-to-Trails program; now there is a walking bridge spanning Otter Creek where the old trestle used to be. On the far side of the bridge you will see the trailhead for the **Scenic Backbone Trail**, which bears an uncanny resemblance to the same feature in Backbone State Park.

The main geologic feature of Echo Valley Park is the one-hundred-foot-high ridge or backbone of Hopkinton dolomite that separates Otter and Glover Creeks—both trout streams. The Backbone is also an ecological wall—the Otter Creek side is sunny and dry, while the Glover Creek side is shaded and wet. The two streams converge beyond the park boundaries.

The cedar-lined Scenic Backbone Trail follows the narrowing ridge to a point where there are just several feet of rock between a precipice on either side. A deep, cavelike chasm rives the bluff at this point, but don't descend here—go back a hundred feet, where you will find an easy descent to the base of the cliff on the sunny, Otter Creek side. Here you will find a huge, moss-covered "float block," or boulder, with a tree growing from the top, and a roomy talus cave beneath. Talus caves are formed in the spaces between boulders.

There are two entrances to the cave—one easy, the other a bit tighter. There is room for several people to sit comfortably within, and it's carpeted with dry oak leaves. The cave is a dozen feet long, five feet high, and has a tight crawlway leading off from the main room that is not recommended for further exploration. The massive rock forming the ceiling rests at a 45-degree angle supported by two mirror-image boulders. White calcite swirls adorn the walls.

Also visit the old limekiln, surrounded by a chain-link fence, along the park road. A sign states that the remnants of a foundation in front of the kiln belong to a gristmill that burned down in 1883. Mortar made in this kiln was used to build houses in West Union and the CCC structures in the park. If you want to visit another cave in the park, walk over to the stream banks adjacent to the kiln. On the opposite bank you will see the round arch of a cave, a rock tube three feet high and about a dozen feet long.

At the entrance to Echo Valley Park, you had a choice of going downhill to the right, into the Otter Creek valley (which has been described above), or uphill to the left, to the **Glover's Creek Access**. The latter road ends at a small picnic area on the creek. Glover's Cave, pictured on old postcards but not visible from the access road, is on private land.

Directions: From U.S. Highway 18 in West Union, take Pine Street south and turn east on Echo Valley Road for 1.8 miles. The park is on the left.

Season/hours: Daily, 4:00 a.m. to 10:30 p.m. Free.

Length: Various.

Precautions: Jacket, gloves, and lights.

Amenities: Picnic tables and pavilion, restrooms, primitive camping.

Contact: Fayette County Conservation Board, 18673 Lane Road, Fayette, IA 52142.
Phone: (563) 422-5146 or -3613.

This cave, situated in reddish Pennsylvanian sandstone on the banks of the Iowa River in Eldora, may be related to former coal mining activities in the area.

14

Eldora Cave
Hardin County

ON THE EAST SIDE of Eldora in Deer Park is a cave worth noting—and easy to get to. Maps of the park trails are posted on large signs, and the cave is clearly marked on them. Deer Park is bisected into northern and southern halves by a steep ravine running down to the Iowa River along the line of 11th Avenue. Follow the gravel trail down through the ravine, crossing the wooden footbridge, until just before the trail reaches the river, then take the narrower trail that branches off to the right, skirting the reddish rock outcrops. After walking several hundred feet you will see wooden steps curving upward to the cave entrance, which is 6 feet high and 20 feet wide. The walk from start to finish is about one-quarter mile, and the trek is well worth the effort because of the view of the river valley from the cave entrance.

The cave is situated in the reddish, Pennsylvanian-age Eldora sandstone, streaked with lime-green lichens. A curious feature is the box work seen in the cave walls, created by differential weathering—resistant layers are left projecting as fins. The cave appears to be very short but holds a surprise at the end. Just when you think you've reached the rear wall, another room comes into view above you. This dark chamber, about eight feet high with standing room only, is accessible but requires a flashlight. Cold air blows from amid the voids. Are there more passages beyond?

Whether the red cave of Eldora is natural or artificial in origin is not readily apparent. It is known, however, that the Eldora Coal Company was active in this area around the time of the Civil War. Could this cave have been the beginning of a coal drift? Although no coal beds are visible in the immediate vicinity, it remains a possibility.

By the way, if you want to take in more of this pleasant town, visit the Owasa Depot, which houses the Eldora Welcome Center and Railroad Museum; the complex is in Deer Park. **Pine Lake State Park** is just across the Iowa River.

Directions: Deer Park is at the intersection of State Highway 175 (Edgington Avenue) and Park Street, on the east side of Eldora.

Season/hours: Daily, 5:00 a.m. to 11:00 p.m. Free.
Length: 20 feet.
Precautions: Lights.
Amenities: Picnic tables, pavilions, playgrounds, deer pen, and the Eldora Welcome Center. Pine Lake State Park is just across the river.
Contact: Eldora Area Chamber and Development Council, 1442 Washington Street, Eldora, IA 50627. Phone: (641) 939-3241. Web site: www.eldoraiowa.com

Wildcat Cave
Hardin County

WILDCAT CAVE, perched in the walls of a red sandstone glen, is a veritable signature gallery of early Iowa settlers. Looking carefully at its walls you can find names and dates going back well into the nineteenth century. But crawling onward through the dusty rock tube, you will find the remains of far earlier inhabitants of Iowa—the giant trees of the Coal Age, represented here by fragments of petrified wood! Casual observers have sometimes mistaken the fossil wood for petrified snakeskin, owing to the diamond pattern of its leaf scars.

The 46-acre access area in which the cave resides is well marked but the cave itself is not. After following the directions below, park your vehicle where indicated and follow the narrow, mowed footpath between the fence lines toward the woods ahead of you, a quarter mile to the south. Upon reaching them, you will find a wooden footbridge at the head of a ravine that leads down to the Iowa River. Take a right and go down the ravine toward the river rather than crossing the footbridge.

Hike down the deep, narrow, and meandering red sandstone canyon. This Pennsylvanian-age rock is the same age as Iowa's coal beds. Make your way among the mossy boulders and fallen timber. Within a few hundred feet the cave will be obvious in a promontory halfway up the left side of the gorge—about 25 feet above the dry streambed. It's an easy scramble to the entrance, but watch for loose

Wildcat Cave, located in the wooded ravine beyond the sign, was a veritable signature gallery for old settlers.

stones on the slope.

The oval entrance to Wildcat Cave is six feet high and four feet wide. The cave runs 30 feet straight into the bluff. The front third, where you can comfortably stand, is where to look for the signatures. The remainder of the cave is a crawlway. It's an easy and comfortable crawl, however, over dry red mud, with a clearance of one and a half feet and a constant cool breeze. At the far end, the passage widens out a bit, but it's not very easy to turn around back there, so you will need to back your way out. This is where you can find the petrified wood.

Upon leaving the cave, if you continue down the red sandstone glen, you will come to the Iowa River. Notice the delta of stones that extends from the ravine halfway out into the river channel. These stones were washed down the ravine during wet weather and deposited at its mouth.

Returning up the glen to the wooden footbridge, the path (usually mowed) continues for quite some distance, marked by a series of wooden posts. You can follow the path to where it approaches the very edge of the river bluff, just beyond the power line that crosses the river. If you are physically fit, you may be able to scramble down the bluff here and find **Rattlesnake Cave**, where additional signatures can be found.

A nearby attraction, just upriver, is **Steamboat Rock**, best seen from Steamboat Rock–Tower Rock County Park in the town of Steamboat Rock. The 60-foot bluff was so named because it was thought to resemble—what else?—a steamboat.

Directions:	From County Road S56, one mile south of the town of Steamboat Rock, watch for the sign for Wildcat Trail. Go west on the gravel road for one mile and then south for a quarter mile. Where the road turns west again there is a sign for Wildcat Cave Access, but the parking area is very small. The cave is in the wooded ravine a quarter mile to the south; follow the easement.
Season/hours:	Daily, 5:00 a.m. to 10:00 p.m. Free.
Length:	30 feet.
Precautions:	Jacket, gloves, and lights.
Amenities:	Hiking.
Contact:	Hardin County Conservation Board, 15537 South Avenue, Ackley, IA 50601. Phone: (641) 648-4361. Web site: www.hardincountyconservation.com/parks

16

Frankenstein Cave
Jackson County

THE OZARK WILDLIFE Area is a butterfly-shaped parcel of land about half a square mile in size along the North Fork of the Maquoketa River, several miles downstream from Searryl's Cave State Preserve. The wildlife area was named after Ozark, a nearby ghost town.

The dirt roads snaking through the wildlife area are marked "Level B Service"—which means they are little better than ruts that are easy to get stuck in during wet weather. So if you don't have four-wheel drive, play it safe and park at one of the lots along the perimeter and hike in.

Rocky ravines—the "magnesian dales" of the old geological surveys—run back from the river, and these are good places to hunt for caves, especially when the leaves are off the trees. Although the streambeds are usually dry, the abundance of flood debris festooning the trees—resembling a yard that has been toilet-papered—as well as the enormous logjams, testify to the occasional torrential floods that pour through this area.

The Ozark rock is covered with tiny solutional sponging—typical of the Hopkinton dolomite—and contains abundant fossils in places. While hiking up one of the streambeds, I found a nice chunk of jasper and what appeared to be a fossilized honeycomb. No, this has nothing to do with bees; they did not exist back in the Silurian Period! The "honeycomb" was an extinct coral that weathers out of the rock. I left it where I found it because, of course, removing specimens from public areas is prohibited.

While there are many rockshelters in the Ozark Wildlife Area, you need to hike around a bit to find an honest-to-goodness cave. Be aware that you may pick your way through the barbed-wire-like bushes only to find a shadow pretending to be a cave. But if you keep your eye on the outcrops, you will eventually see, at a bend in one of the valleys, a beetling bluff that resembles the head of Frankenstein. Nearby is a large cave entrance.

The main room of Frankenstein Cave is about the size of a tool shed. An animal trap suggests that the cave is well known to the locals. At the far end of the room is a large boulder and, behind it, a rocky passage sloping down. A more intense caving experience begins here for those who are interested. If you do forge ahead, note that you may be greeted by the musty odor and abundance of raccoon scats, thus facing the possibility of confronting one of the occupants in the close confines of the crawlway. After about a dozen feet, the passage opens into a wide space a little over a foot high that contains a few stalagmites. This is a good place to turn around and head back to the entrance.

On my first visit to this remote and scenic wildlife area, I asked a friendly farmer at the Caven Bridge Access—presumably the name Caven is pure coincidence—for directions. He assumed that I was a mushroom hunter. When I told him that I was instead hunting for caves, he told me about the nearby **Ozark Spring Cave**, which the discoverers of Coldwater Cave had attempted to dive in the 1960s. Unfortunately, this cave isn't part of the wildlife area.

Directions: From County Road Y31 (Bernard Road) south of Garry Owen, go west on 234th Street to a T-junction at 21st Avenue. Go south on 21st. You will pass the Ozark Cemetery and come to a bridge over the North Fork of the Maquoketa River. Just before the bridge, on the left side, you will see a gravel road and a sign for the Ozark Wildlife Area. Follow the road along the river for 0.8 mile, where you will find a sign marked "Pedestrian Traffic Only" at the mouth of a ravine. Frankenstein Cave is located a quarter mile up the ravine, on the right side, where the stream makes a bend.

Season/hours: Daily, 4:00 a.m. to 10:30 p.m. Free.

Length: Various.

Precautions: Jacket, gloves, and lights. Some of the "roads" are little better than deep ruts—avoid them during wet weather or altogether if your car has low clearance. Wear blaze orange during hunting season.

Amenities: Hiking.

Contact: Jackson County Conservation Board, 201 West Platt Street, Maquoketa, IA 52060. Phone: (563) 652-3181.

Maquoketa Caves State Park
Jackson County

EARLY ACCOUNTS of this part of Iowa described "a small wonderland" known as Burt's Caves, later dubbed Morehead's Caves. Early visitors mentioned the "milk-white stalactites" that adorned the caves, long since snatched away by greedy souvenir hunters. The area was a popular picnicking spot long before it became a state park in 1921, when it was renamed Maquoketa Caves. The whole park was added to the National Register of Historic Places in 1991.

The caves in the park were used by Native Americans, as indicated by archeological finds. The recorded history of the caves began in 1837, when two hunters chased a herd of deer up the Raccoon Creek valley from the Maquoketa River. When they saw the deer enter what is now the lower entrance of Dancehall Cave, they concluded that the deer were trapped in the cave and could be taken at leisure. Later, however, they found that the deer had long since just walked out the other side—the upper entrance of the cave.

Maquoketa Caves State Park is a microcosm of the different cave types found in Iowa. To learn more about the caves you should first visit the interpretive kiosk near the main (lower) parking lot. There, a display informs you that there are four types of caves in the park: solutional caves, like Dancehall Cave; mechanical caves, like Fat Man's Misery; talus caves, like Shinbone Cave; and rockshelters, like Twin Arches. Cave maps are also posted here.

The more than one dozen caves in the park are neatly divided into Upper and Lower Valley caves by the road that bisects the park. It is thought that many of these caves, in the distant past, were actually side passages in the hypothetical ancestor of Dancehall Cave, which began to develop less than half a million years ago in the Hopkinton dolomite. Collapse of the big mother cave—which probably had an appearance similar to modern Coldwater Cave—left them isolated as separate caves. These caves, which have undergone several name changes in the past, are located along a good trail with boardwalks and are conveniently identified, including the degree of difficulty. When you see a cave with a crawling caver logo, for example, expect the cave to be more challenging than usual. Beginning with Dancehall

Cave, the caves are described below in clockwise order as they appear along the trail.

Dancehall Cave, the feature attraction of the park, is 1,100 feet long, making it the longest wild cave in Iowa open to the public. It has three entrances: Upper, Middle, and Lower. The cave is easy to walk through, with a passage 20 feet wide and up to 40 feet high, but there are places where adults will need to stoop a bit. Raccoon Creek flows through the cave, and even though there are walkways, expect to get your feet wet. The main passage has a lighting system; however, bring your own lights because the lighting is rather dim, not always turned on, and more important, you may want to explore the side passages, which are totally dark. This cave is closed to the public in winter to protect hibernating bats. As many as 3,000 bats have been seen to emerge from the cave at once, a miniature version of the great bat flights at Carlsbad Caverns in New Mexico.

A long boardwalk stairway leads from the parking lot down to the **Upper Entrance**; the cliff here was formerly a favorite spot for rappelling practice until the practice was banned owing to the severe damage it causes to delicate cliff habitats. From the cave entrance, you can see the **Natural Bridge** just upstream, once part of the cave roof, arching 50 feet above the stream. It is supposedly the largest natural bridge in the Midwest.

Enter Dancehall Cave and follow the passage until it makes an elbow bend, where you will find the entrance to the **Bat Passage** on the right side. Much smaller than the main passage, Bat Passage is a rock tube containing deep pools of cold, muddy water. Even though it loops back to the main cave beyond the elbow, you will need to return the way you came because the opening at the other end is 10 feet above the ground—too high to jump down.

Beyond the elbow in the main passage, you come to the **Middle Entrance**—the part of the cave where the roof has collapsed—complete with its own stairway leading back up to the parking lot. This immense sinkhole is sometimes called **Devil's Cavern**. On the right side there is a large, flat area and the entrance to **Steel Gate Passage**, the most decorated passage in the park and a big favorite with people who crave a more intense caving experience. The passage corkscrews through the rocks for more than two hundred feet, with cave formations as thick as tree trunks. Do not attempt to explore this passage, however, unless you are in good physical condition and willing to get very dirty. Otherwise, follow the passage until you get to the loop and chimney at the far end, and return the same way you came.

Continue beyond the Middle Entrance and you can exit Dancehall Cave at the **Lower Entrance**. By the way, the origin of the name Dancehall Cave remains in dispute. Whether the "dancehall" was a large room in the cave itself or a separate, man-made structure is

Fat Man's Misery, a mechanical cave in Maquoketa Caves State Park, is not as threatening as its name suggests.

sometimes debated.

Just beyond the Lower Entrance, on the left, is **Tourist's Delight Cave**, historically known as Big Spring, but it is closed to the public for very good reasons. Despite the inviting name, it is by far the least tourist-friendly cave in the whole park. A long, tight, nasty mud crawl leads to a passage containing the last of the "milk-white stalactites" beloved by the early settlers, as well as some splendid popcorn formations.

Now you come to the Lower Valley caves. The first is **Rainy Day Cave**, a spring cave with a stream meandering about in a deep groove on its mud floor. Going upstream in the cave, you can't avoid getting your feet wet, and the passage pinches down toward the back end for a length of 90 feet. A short, upper-level passage, 30 feet long, is inaccessible without climbing gear.

Fat Man's Misery is the park's best example of a mechanical cave, in which part of the cliff has detached, leaving a gap to walk through. A stone stairway leads up to the cave, but despite its name, there is ample room to walk and no chance of getting stuck.

When you get to **Ice Cave**, don't expect to find ice! The downward sloping passage does trap cool air, however, affording welcome relief on a hot summer day. The cave contains a dome room with a 25-foot ceiling that is wet and drippy. Stalagmite stumps cover the floor. The passage tapers down to a stoop way and ends in a sit-up room, for a total length of 123 feet.

Crossing over to the opposite side of Raccoon Creek, you will see what appears to be the impressive entrance to **Shinbone Cave**—a huge opening in the cliff 20 feet high. But as you get closer, the entrance proves to be false, and the "real" cave entrance comes into view—a little hole on the right side of the larger cavity. That hole leads to a corkscrew crawlway, 76 feet long, that parallels the bluff. This is the park's best example of a talus cave—the result of rubble falling from the bluff above and creating a cave that is really only the interconnected space inside a jumble of boulders. This talus cave is completely dark, however, so bring a flashlight and get ready to scrape your shins.

To visit **Barbell Cave** you may need a friend to boost you up to the slightly elevated entrance, which has been polished smooth by countless bodies sliding over it. The cave, shaped like a barbell, consists of two rooms connected by a tight, wet pinch, for a total length of 80 feet. The room beyond the pinch contains pristine flowstone, probably because it's difficult for visitors to reach. Upon leaving the cave, you pass the 17-ton **Balanced Rock**, which rests on a base only a foot in diameter!

Wye Cave is a different kettle of fish altogether. Here, you enter through a sinkhole on top of a hill rather than through a horizontal entrance in the side of a bluff as with the other caves. Do not attempt to explore this cave unless you are in good physical condition and willing to get very dirty. It is most easily reached from the upper parking lot, where there is a convenient water spigot to wash off the mud after leaving the cave. Climbing down through the sinkhole, you find yourself on a steep boulder slope in a big room. Wood is scattered about, even on high ledges, where it was left by storm waters. Climb down over the boulders to the bottom of the room, where you will find a tight pinch about a foot high, through which water drains. Beyond this pinch is the other half of the cave, which is of walking height. Wye Cave is 475 feet long and shaped like the letter Y on a map.

There are seven Upper Valley caves, most of them small. **Window Cave** has a rock "window" from which you can look out into the valley. The interior is of standing height, irregular in shape, and 30 feet long. **Match Cave** is a hard, red, mud crawlway 1 to 3 feet high and 39 feet long. The best part about it is the beautiful boardwalk stairway leading up to the entrance! Crossing Raccoon Creek and continuing along the trail, you next come to **Wide Mouth Cave**, located up a side ravine in the valley. The cave consists of three low rooms and 100 feet of passage. It contains much dead flowstone nowadays, but early accounts tell of its beauty. In winter, the cave often contains a forest of ice stalagmites.

A boardwalk hugs the cliff along the next segment. First comes **Twin Arches**, a rockshelter of standing height and 35 feet long. With two entrances, it has been compared, when viewed from the outside, to a big nose on the side of the cliff—with two flaring nostrils! **Hernandos Hideaway Cave** is an uninviting, knobby rock tube, 39 feet long, ending in a small room. Kneepads are essential on this kind of surface. **Up-N-Down Cave** is so called because you go up into its entrance then down through a hole two feet wide into a dome of standing height for a length of 27 feet. The entrance to this cave is small and easily overlooked. Finally, **Dug Out Cave**, 25 feet long, is located in the abutments of the Natural Bridge. The rock is polished smooth and is slippery with mud, so do not attempt to reach this cave if you are unsure of your footing.

To complete your visit to the park, visit **Sagers Museum**, the stone building just outside the park gate, open on summer weekends. From 1925 to 1936, the renowned amateur archeologist Paul Sagers (1909–1982) amassed a huge assortment of artifacts that he dug from rockshelters along the Maquoketa River, a collection that is important to our understanding of Woodland Indian cultures. He operated the museum for 30 years and then donated it to the state. Here you also will find more information about the geology of the caves and take a narrated video tour of the park.

If your interests extend to industrial archeology, visit the huge **Hurstville Lime Kilns** on U.S. Highway 61, two miles north of the town of Maquoketa. In 1870, Alfred Hurst founded the Maquoketa lime industry, which supplied mortar and plaster throughout the Midwest. A company town named Hurstville was built to house immigrants from the country of Luxembourg who worked in the dolomite quarries located along the Maquoketa River. The kilns consumed so many trees that the lime industry was responsible for clearing much of the farmland in Jackson County. The introduction of Portland cement, however, reduced the demand for lime, and Hurstville became a ghost town. The four 24-foot-tall kilns are on the National Register of Historic Places.

Directions:	From U.S. Highway 61 at the town of Maquoketa, go west on County Road Y31 (Caves Road) for six miles; it goes right past the park entrance.
Season/hours:	Daily, 4:00 a.m. to 10:30 p.m. Dancehall Cave is closed in winter to protect hibernating bats. Free.
Length:	Various.
Precautions:	Jacket, gloves, and lights. The walkways in Dancehall Cave are wet. Full caving gear is recommended for the Steel Gate Passage of Dancehall Cave and for Wye Cave.
Amenities:	Picnic tables, pavilions, and campground with showers. A water faucet at the upper parking lot allows you to wash off after caving.
Contact:	Maquoketa Caves State Park, RR 2, Maquoketa, IA 52060. Phone: (563) 652-5833. Web site: www.state.ia.us/parks

18

Werden's Cave
Jackson County

APPROACHING WERDEN'S CAVE is like approaching the dwelling of a hobbit in Middle Earth. The low entrance is found in a craggy rock outcrop surrounded by oak trees with twisted arms. The cave is a 700-foot-long maze in Hopkinton dolomite and is one of those magical places where it's okay to tell your kids to "get lost." Not to worry, tours are conducted under the watchful eye of a county conservation naturalist. Adults are also welcome and will enjoy the cave just as much as the kids. I sure did!

Crawl through the opening at the foot of the cliff and enter the Big Room—the hub of the Werden maze, created by artesian waters. The 10-foot ceiling is pockmarked with solutional holes. From here, you can venture forth in several directions. Visit the Dragon's Lair, a small room off to one side, or peer into the Belfry, a small dome. Beyond the Belfry, the passage slopes uphill under a sinkhole where you can see tree roots dangling down from above. Send the children through the Birth Canal, about one foot in diameter—adults will not fit!

The next big room resembles a cleared forest. The broken stumps of stalagmites are mute testimony to the depredations of vandals in former times. The red mud floor is cratered with archeological test pits. Continue to the Foothills Room, which contains a supervised climbing challenge—Black Hawk's Chimney—and a pretty little flowstone grotto off to one side. That should prepare you for the Rocky Mountain Room, which, true to its name, contains a jumble of boulders piled high into the air. You then descend by way of the Mudslide. You can return to the Big Room by way of the tight Mousetrap passage—again, just large enough for kids.

It's very likely that you will see bats whizzing about during your visit. The eastern pipistrelle bat, less common than other species of bat in Iowa, is almost exclusively the kind that hibernates here in winter, when the cave is off-limits.

Note that Werden's (frequently spelled "Worden's") Cave is located on private property, and tours can be arranged only through the Clinton County Conservation Board—even though the cave is physically located in Jackson County. Tours depart from the Eden Valley Nature Center (see below for more information). The center has rocks, minerals, fossils, and wildlife displays. Be sure to check out the

Werden's Cave, a 700-foot artesian maze, is a favorite with children. But note that the cave is on private property and can be visited only by arranging a tour with the Clinton County Conservation Board.

center's vivarium for the tiger salamanders—a species that also inhabits Werden's Cave. The salamander retains a fat store in its tail for hibernation. The center offers bat-house building workshops, among its many other programs.

The nature center sits in a web of gravel hiking trails in the scenic Eden Valley Refuge, through which Bear Creek flows. You may want to hike the trail that leads to **Wulf's Den**, passing by way of the Great Stone Face, a curiously shaped rock outcrop that recalls the famous short story by Nathaniel Hawthorne. The den, however, is named after a former landowner, Arnold Wulf—not the animal. Wulf dynamited a cellar into the bluff and used it for cold storage. A wooden stairway along the trail leads up to the gate (usually open) in the bluff. The rock chamber, which has standing room for several people, contains an abundance of "devil's claws," also called "fossil pig's feet," in its ceiling. Technically, they are known as pentamerid brachiopods.

Directions: The Eden Valley Nature Center, from which tours to the cave depart, is located on County Road Y32 (50th Avenue), two miles south of Baldwin.

Season/hours: Tours of Werden's Cave are only available through the Clinton County Conservation Board, and the cave is closed entirely from October 31 to April 1 to protect hibernating bats. The Eden Valley Nature Center is open Saturdays, 1:00 to 4:00 from May to October. Scheduled events are free to all. Tours by appointment are free to residents of Clinton County, and out-of-county groups are charged a blanket fee of $80.

Length: 700 feet.

Precautions: Full caving gear, including kneepads, is recommended. Hard hats are provided. Expect to get muddy.

Amenities: Campground, hiking trails.

Contact: Clinton County Conservation Board, P.O. Box 68, Grand Mound, IA 52751. Phone: (563) 847-7202. Web site: www.clintoncountyiowa.com

19

Camp Wyoming
Jones County

WHO WOULD have thought that Camp Wyoming, the main Presbyterian camp and conference center for eastern Iowa, once harbored horse thieves? This 38-acre wooded camp is bisected by Bear Creek, along which lie four named caves in the Silurian dolomite outcrops. Three of them, including Horsethief Cave, are located fairly close to one another, in the vicinity of Cedar Point. The cave locations are marked on the campground maps and require some hiking to get to. If you want to camp and cave at the same time, however, Camp Wyoming is an ideal place for you. It is privately owned but everyone is welcome.

Horsethief Cave is the largest, best marked, and most accessible of the Camp Wyoming caves. You don't even need a flashlight to explore it. It's located on the south bank of Bear Creek, directly in line with the narrow swinging bridge that spans the stream. Cross the bridge and follow the wooden stairway leading up to the big entrance on the other side. The cave passage, about 50 feet long, tapers down and turns a corner at the back end. A small amount of flowstone and popcorn coats the walls.

Over the years, Horsethief Cave has provided a colorful backdrop for entertaining and instructing the regular patrons of Camp Wyoming. A fire pit marks the entrance, with convenient benchlike boulders to sit on, and the dry floor of the cave is carpeted with leaves. The cave faces west, offering nice views at sunset. At the site, children are entertained with tales of the namesake horse thieves who reputedly hid their booty here. In keeping with the spooky surroundings, stories are also spun about the early Christian catacombs, an image reinforced by planting candles among the cave's rock ledges. That accounts for the splatters of wax all over the place!

Fatman's Misery Cave is located about a hundred feet upstream from Horsethief Cave. Starting at the foot of the Horsethief Cave stairway, follow a faint footpath along the south bank of Bear Creek until you get to this small talus cave, formed in the voids between boulders at the base of the bluff. There are two entrances. The lower one, which is rather tight, is a small, triangular opening. If you enter here, you will have to belly crawl 10 feet up a steep mud slope into the

Big Spring

There are many big springs in the karst country of Iowa, but one in particular, located on the Turkey River in Clayton County, is the granddaddy of them all. Big Spring, which issues from the Galena dolomite, has an average flow rate of 15,000 gallons per minute and, based on underground dye traces, drains an area of one hundred square miles.

Beginning in the late 1930s, Big Spring was the site of a trout farm and fishing club. A dam was built around the spring to raise the water level and rearing ponds were dug. In winter, the ponds were used as skating rinks, with electric lights for night skating. Ice was cut on the nearby Turkey River and used to pack the trout. Because of runoff from agricultural land, however, the spring spewed vast quantities of silt—nearly a hundred tons per hour during storms—which suffocated the trout eggs and required endless dredgings of ponds and race-ways. Indeed, there was so much silt that it was utilized as a construction material around the hatchery. The owners, not realizing at first how karst systems operate, thought they could solve the silt problem by capping sinkholes on the uplands that drained to the spring—only to find that the water very soon found another route! The Turkey River would also sometimes rise unexpectedly and overflow the hatchery, mixing the different sizes of trout together or sweeping them away entirely.

The state purchased Big Spring in 1961 but, because of the silt problem, decided to use it only as a rearing station. Spawning was moved to the Manchester hatchery. Disaster struck in 1963. A cheese company emptied its whey pond and the waste traveled 14 miles underground to Big Spring. All oxygen was sucked from the water, killing more than a hundred thousand trout.

In the 1980s, the Big Spring basin was chosen by the Iowa Geological Survey as an ideal place to study how pollution from agricultural activities affects water quality. The major contaminants are bacteria, pesticides, and nitrates from fertilizers.

Big Spring Hatchery stocks trout for northeastern Iowa. It is located at 16212 Big Spring Road, northwest of Elkader. Free guided tours are available; call (563) 245-2446.

sit-up room. An easier way to enter is by the upper entrance, which also serves as a skylight for the cave. The entire venture should convince you that Fatman's Misery lives up to its name! Plan to get dirty.

Mystery Cave, certainly the most complex cave at Camp Wyoming, is located a half mile downstream from Horsethief Cave. From the swinging bridge, follow the mowed path along the north bank of Bear Creek. You will see the cave's keyhole-shaped entrance about 20 feet up in the cliff, but it's easy to get to. The cave is a three-dimensional maze with a total length of 50 feet, and its bone-white walls are adorned with popcorn. The passages curve back on themselves, which perhaps inspired the cave's name. There is no chance of getting lost, but you'll definitely need a light to explore this one.

Bobcat Cave is located by itself at the west end of the camp, near the Tree Chapel. Follow the steep footpath leading down the bluff behind the Cardinal Cabin, and walk one hundred feet upstream along the outcrops on the north bank of Bear Creek. The entrance to the cave is a three-foot high Gothic-like opening flanked on either side by dead trees, about 20 feet above the stream. The cave is a rock tube—perhaps an old spring exit. The crawlway, which has a mud floor, meanders for about 30 feet, following a joint, before tapering down and ending in a welter of coon scat.

Directions:	From State Highway 64, two miles east of the town of Wyoming ("The Christmas City"), you will see a sign for the camp. Go a half mile south on the gravel road (42nd Avenue) to the camp gate.
Season/hours:	Open year round. Fee for the use of campgrounds.
Length:	Various.
Precautions:	Jacket, gloves, and lights.
Amenities:	Full campground with showers, primitive and electric sites. Camp Wyoming has conference facilities.
Contact:	Camp Wyoming, 9106 42nd Avenue, Wyoming, IA 52362. Phone: (563) 488-3893. Web site: www.jonescountytourism.com/parks/campwyoming.html

20

Indian Bluff Cave
Jones County

INDIAN BLUFF CAVE is so popular—especially with kids from the neighboring youth camps—that the rocky walls of the cave have actually been worn smooth here and there by the passage of countless bodies! At 525 feet, this is perhaps the longest wild cave open to the public in a county park. And because it consists of just a single passage, there's no chance of getting lost.

From the very beginning, as you drive downhill along the curving gravel road into **Pictured Rocks County Park**, you see what appear to be inviting voids in the bluffs on both sides of the road. Don't be distracted—they are merely shadows pretending to be caves. Erosion has sculpted these bluffs to resemble rows of moss-covered ship's hulls. On both sides of the road at the bottom of the hill, there are large rockshelters in the outcrops. This park is a favorite place for rock climbers, judging from all the bolts in the cliffs.

Continue down onto the floodplain of the Maquoketa River; to the right is the campground, and to the left is Indian Bluff Cave. Turn left and drive to the gravel lot. Follow the trail a quarter mile upstream along the bluffs. You will see interesting rockshelters along the way, some of which have archeological significance. Notice the abundance of black springs, mosses, and ferns on the scenic outcrops. The ferns sprout from small amounts of soil in the vugs, or pockets, in the Hopkinton dolomite. At the end of the trail you will find a railroad-tie stairway leading up to the cave, which is located at the foot of a cedar-crowned bluff. Geologically, the cave is unusual in that it is a fairly linear passage in a type of rock that usually favors maze caves.

A few caveats: The cave entrance is 6 feet high and 15 feet wide but rapidly tapers to a crawlway. The cave requires substantial crawling, and kneepads are highly recommended to guard against the sharp gravel and rock protuberances. Also, this cave is not for seriously overweight individuals or for those with any hint of claustrophobia.

A stiff wind—sometimes enough to snuff out candles—blows through the entrance rooms. You will pass several rock joints at right angles to the passage—places where you can see high up into narrow cracks. The walls are covered with cave popcorn. If you visit during

The steps lead to Indian Bluff Cave, whose rock walls have been polished smooth by countless visitors.

the winter, you may encounter a strange ice formation about one hundred feet inside. Water dripping from the ceiling at this point often freezes to form an image resembling an "ice medusa," complete with ringlets represented by stalactites hanging around the circumference. Thereafter you come to a fork in the passage, but the two resulting passages come back together after a short distance. The passage to the left is tighter. Beyond the point where they rejoin you encounter a series of sharp, hairpin bends in the passage—narrow enough that you might have to turn sideways to get through some of them.

Now that you're past the worst of the crawling you can resume walking. About halfway through the cave, you'll find the so-called Standing-Up Room. But don't stop there—the best is yet to come. Continue on another couple hundred feet to where the passage appears to dead-end. On the right-hand side, you will find that it actually continues, doubling back into a low crawlway 30 feet long. Just beyond is Gietkowski's Grotto, the largest room in the cave, enough to hold ten people comfortably. Now, finally, you've reached the end!

Directions: From Monticello, take State Highway 38 south for two miles and turn east on 190th Street. Go two miles to where the blacktop ends and the road descends a hill. Don't confuse the park with the similarly named Pictured Rocks Camp.

Season/hours: Open year round, 4:30 a.m. to 10:30 p.m. Free.

Length: 525 feet.

Precautions: Bring full caving gear. Kneepads are a must, due to the sharp gravel on the floor of the passages. Not for seriously overweight individuals.

Amenities: Picnic tables, restrooms, campground.

Contact: Jones County Conservation Board, 12515 Central Park Road, Center Junction, IA 52212. Phone: (563) 487-3541. Web site: www.monticello.ia.us/RecTourism/#PicturedRocks

21

Searryl's Cave State Preserve
Jones County

SEARRYL'S CAVE provides vivid experiences that visitors will remember for a lifetime: spooky auditory effects, great twin domes, gluey, red, boot-sucking mud, and waist-deep water— colored a beautiful aquamarine, but intensely cold. If all this doesn't appeal to you, you won't like Searryl's Cave.

Before Searryl's Cave became a state preserve, landowner relations were very ugly. Jim Hedges, one of Iowa's legendary cavers, wrote in 1974, "Going to this cave is a good way to get shot on sight." He wasn't kidding!

The preserve in which the cave resides, named after the original homesteader, is located along the scenic bluffs of the North Fork of the Maquoketa River. To get there, you need to follow an easement through a half mile of farmland. From the rather obscure parking area along the gravel road, walk past the gate and head north toward the woods. (A sign on the gate appears to have a lightning bolt scrawled on it. In fact, it represents the zigzag route of the easement you're supposed to follow through the fields!) During harvest time, it may seem as if you're threading a vast corn maze. When you reach the edge of the woods you will encounter a barbed-wire fence; look for the gate in this fence and follow the faint footpath leading downhill to the cave.

Once you're there, the mouth of the cave appears, crescent-shaped, 50 feet wide and 2 feet high, in a horseshoe-shaped overhang of Hopkinton dolomite. A waterfall notch, usually dry, indents the over- hang. A sign reminds you that entry is prohibited between October 15 and April 1 because of bat hibernation. Reportedly, Searryl's has the largest wintering bat population in Iowa.

Although the entrance is low and unimpressive, the interior is oth- erwise. Descend the mud slope to the lake in the entrance room. This is where you should turn back unless you have adequate cave gear, including chest waders, because the cold water can be rather deep at times. If you continue upstream wearing the proper gear, you'll find that the water gets deeper and the passage curves to the right and

Searryl's Cave, haunted by "cave fairies," is closed from October to April to protect hibernating bats.

heads into darkness. At the first bend, you can crawl up onto the mud bank and see a vast "pancake" room—so called because of its low, flat roof. It seems to go on forever. Do not crawl through this room, however, because you will endanger the delicate soda straws and popcorn that adorn its ceiling. This is also where you may encounter the "cave fairies." Ah yes, those!

In describing the strange sounds many people hear inside this cave, Hedges wrote, "The cave fairies, ah, the cave fairies. Whistling, warbling, twittering, twaddling, giggling, gurgling, limpidly laughing little girls' voices." He was not alone in that perception. During my own visit, it sounded as if there was a group of cavers approaching through the stream passage, chatting noisily as they walked. My first thought was, "Why can't I see their lights?" The voices vanished as I proceeded upstream, however. The creepy sound effects are generated by dripping water.

Reentering the stream by way of a mud chute, you arrive at the first big dome, 30 feet high and 50 feet in diameter. You can ascend from the stream into the dome itself by climbing the high banks of red, layered clay; look for the deep foot ruts, worn by generations of Iowa cavers. On the floor of the dome, several areas of pure white calcite are taped off; you are not allowed to walk there. One of them protects a nest of cave pearls that formed under the main drip of the dome.

Reentering the stream and walking upstream toward the second dome, you will need to stoop because of the low ceiling. Bats may whiz past your ears. The second dome, about the same size and shape as the first, is wetter, and this mud has the consistency of peanut butter: Hedges referred to it as "gloop." Upstream from the second dome the passage becomes a muddy, miserable crawlway that dwindles down to nothing, and there's no point in getting soaked. Return the way you came. Upon leaving the cave, you might want to go down and take a bath in the Maquoketa River!

Directions: From the intersection of State Highways 64 and 136 in the community of Wyoming, go north on 136 for 12.6 miles to Temple Hill Road (County Road D65). Turn right (east) to St. Peter's Church. Go north on 202nd Street for 1.8 miles to Skahill Road, then south 2.5 miles to the posted gate on the north side of the road. There is walk-in access only, a total distance of three-quarters of a mile. Head toward the wooded river valley following the easement through the farm field.

Season/hours: Daily, 4:00 a.m. to 10:30 p.m. Cave entry prohibited between October 15 and April 1 because of bat hibernation. Free.

Length: 565 feet.

Precautions: Jacket, gloves, and lights. For anything beyond the entrance room, however, full caving gear, including waders or wetsuit, is recommended. This cave, except for the entrance room, is not for children.

Amenities: Hiking.

Contact: IDNR, Wapsipinicon State Park, RR 2, Anamosa, IA 52205. Phone: (319) 462-2761. Web site: www.state.ia.us/parks

Wapsipinicon State Park
Jones County

IN 1922, Horsethief Cave, in the newly established Wapsipinicon State Park, was being developed as a tourist attraction. After the smoke had cleared from an explosion to remove a large boulder from the cave, inmates from the nearby Anamosa Reformatory, who were being pressed into service as laborers, returned to continue their work. Upon reaching the cave, they were astonished to see bones littering the floor. An amateur archeologist was hastily called in, and he excavated nine human skeletons, all buried in a sitting position, facing the entrance! He reported darkly that "much evidence of cannibalism

The stairway leads to the Ice Cave on Dutch Creek, Wapsipinicon State Park.

was found throughout the cave." The skeletons were later estimated to be four thousand years old. The case attracted nationwide attention to the park—as did the enormous Ku Klux Klan rally held there a few years later.

Wapsipinicon State Park is the site of several accessible caves, but **Horsethief Cave**, located on Dutch Creek, a tributary of the Wapsipinicon River, is the most noteworthy. To get to the cave, park at the stone bridge over Dutch Creek and walk a few hundred feet upstream to the wooden stairway that curves up to the huge mouth of the cave, which measures 15 feet high and 30 feet across. Large, geodelike voids ornament its craggy walls, which some visitors unfortunately seem to regard as convenient trash receptacles. The cave, one hundred feet long, funnels down to a mere slot at the back end. Squeeze through the slot and you'll see a yellow mud bank where, at least at the time of my visit, it appeared as if someone had been digging. You can also visit **Luna Cave**, a 25-foot crawlway just to the right of the entrance of Horsethief Cave.

Ice Cave, also on Dutch Creek, is very different from Horsethief Cave. This cave is reached by ascending a short flight of concrete steps. The narrow rock tube's cross section is shaped like a keyhole, and when the sun shines down the passage, you can see some interesting lighting effects. Toward the end of this 72-foot cave, where the walls are ribbed with flowstone ledges, the passage gets very tight.

Buffalo Den is the big, easy-to-spot rockshelter on the bluffs of the Wapsipinicon River, just downstream from the boat ramp. Follow the trail up the slope, which is often carpeted with wildflowers. The shelter is 30 feet high, 20 feet wide, and 42 feet long, and is floored with red sand. At the left corner of the shelter there is a square, four-by-four-foot natural chimney—the only dark place—which goes 20 feet straight up into the bluff. This chimney, which corresponds with a sinkhole on the top of the bluff, dumps water into the shelter during rain.

In addition to the caves described above, there are many other little tubes and rockshelters in the Silurian dolomite bluffs of Wapsipinicon State Park, bearing names found only in obscure caving publications. An example is **Snow Cave**, a crevice that comfortably fits just one person—lying down! It's located at the top of the talus slope just to the left of the stairway near the pavilions on the Wapsipinicon River. You can have fun hunting for the rest!

Wapsipinicon State Park is in the heart of Grant Wood country. Wood, an artist known for his rolling landscape paintings of Iowa, established an art colony in nearby **Stone City**, where you can get a glimpse (at least from a distance) of underground limestone mines—in addition to the vast surface quarries. The Stone City quarries provided the stone from which the Anamosa Penitentiary and many other Iowa buildings were constructed.

To experience a "hole" of another sort, visit the nearby **Anamosa Penitentiary Museum**, where you can explore a replica cell, see prison artifacts, and view the rap sheets of notorious alumni. The museum is open Friday, Saturday, and Sunday from noon to 4:00 p.m., April–October; other times by appointment. Call (800) 383-0831. Fee.

Directions:	Located on U.S. Highway 151 at south edge of Anamosa.
Season/hours:	Daily, 4:00 a.m. to 10:30 p.m. Free.
Length:	Various.
Precautions:	Getting to some caves requires ascending steep slopes.
Amenities:	Picnicking, fishing, boating, golf.
Contact:	Wapsipinicon State Park, RR 2, Anamosa, IA 52205. Phone: (319) 462-2761. Web site: www.state.ia.us/parks

23

Mosquito Cave
Linn County

T HE MOST LEGENDARY cave in Cedar Rapids is **Horsethief Cave** located on the banks of Indian Creek near Mount Calvary Cemetery. After the Civil War, the story goes, a gang of horse thieves used to run their stolen horses through the cave, emerging near Anamosa—23 miles away! The limestone outcrop, one of the few in the vicinity, was later used as a quarry, and the cave entrance was filled with rubble. The cave was dug open several times—once by boy scouts—and 210 feet of passage were explored. Steve Barnett, co-discoverer of Coldwater Cave (see the description later in this section), spent a lot of time digging at Horsethief Cave before moving on to his greater find. However, the cave, which sits on private property, is again sealed. If you're planning to go underground in Cedar Rapids, Mosquito Cave is your best bet.

Mosquito Cave, located in Jones Park, is found in a low outcrop of Devonian limestone on the banks of Prairie Creek near its junction

Mosquito Cave, on the banks of Prairie Creek in Jones Park, Cedar Rapids, is full of raccoon bones.

with the Cedar River. The entrance to the cave is 10 feet wide and 2 feet high. Because it's located on a floodplain, the floor of the cave may be muddy in the spring, so wear gloves. Beyond the entrance, which contains a lot of driftwood, the passage veers off to the left and gets lower, for a total length of 27 feet. The roof contains a groove— probably a vestige of the embryonic cave itself. The cave is a veritable ossuary of animal skulls and bones, giving you some idea of the various denizens of Iowa's underground regions. It's unclear whether Mosquito Cave was named for its size or for the insects, which do indeed seem to abound here!

Directions: Mosquito Cave is located in the southeastern corner of Jones Park in Cedar Rapids. From the parking lot at the Tait Cummins Sports Complex (north of the big power station) walk north along C Street to the bridge over Prairie Creek. Walk upstream along the north side of the stream about 100 feet until reaching a low rock outcrop. The cave entrance is at ground level.

Season/hours: While the park is open year round, the cave may be flooded and inaccessible during high water in the spring. Free.

Length: 27 feet.

Precautions: Jacket, gloves, and lights.

Amenities: Jones Park has picnic grounds and a golf course. The Cedar Rapids Trail is nearby.

Contact: Cedar Rapids Parks Department, 3601 42nd Street NE, Cedar Rapids, IA 52403.
Phone: (319) 286-5760.
Web site: www.cedar-rapids.org/parks

24

Palisades-Kepler State Park
Linn County

JAMES SHERMAN MINOTT was a Civil War veteran who made his home in a cave along the Cedar River. He lived by fishing, hunting, and trapping and was fond of giving bizarre names to the natural features around him—names like Blow Out Hollow and Screeching Sands Hollow. In the late 1890s he bought land on the river and built a general store, hotel, restaurant, and boat livery. He sold lots for summer cottages and played a key role in making the Palisades of the Cedar River a popular recreation area. However, it wasn't until 1922, a decade after Minott died, that the Palisades became a state park, to which the Louis Kepler Memorial Area was added a few years later. The poet Carl Sandburg and his Cornell College students frequently picnicked in the park.

The Palisades themselves are sheer cliffs of Silurian dolomite, named after the famous Palisades along the Hudson River in New York State. While there are plenty of caves in Palisades-Kepler State Park, most of them can only be reached by boat. It's possible for land-lubbers to visit this park and not even realize there are caves here. But you can see a few of them honeycombing the Palisades on the western side of the Cedar River by driving down to the river via the main park access road (which is on the eastern side of the river).

Given the sheer cliffs, the Palisades-Kepler caves are extremely difficult to approach from the landward side. And don't attempt to swim across the Cedar River to get to them—signs on the beach warn of dangerous currents. The dam, built by the Civilian Conservation Corps for recreational purposes, washed out shortly after it was built and was never adequately repaired. The breach in the dam funnels the river, creating a deadly vortex. There are a few small rockshelters near the dam itself.

The best strategy is to bring a canoe and head across the river to **Shelter Cave**, the big and very noticeable cavity in the bluff near the private stone cottage perched nearly above it. The cottage was originally built for Howard Hall, a wealthy industrialist from Cedar Rapids. Because the cave looked like it was created from the impact of a cannonball, Minott gave the name Blow Out Hollow to the wooded

Shelter Cave, which can be reached only by boat on the Cedar River at Palisades-Kepler State Park, was the inspiration for the name given to Blow Out Hollow, a nearby scenic ravine.

ravine located in the state preserve just south of the cottage.

Shelter Cave has two levels, with 55 feet of passage. Just to the left of it is **Coon Cave**, a 40-foot crawlway, and to the right is **Log Cave**, a 25-foot crawlway. Between the cottage and the dam, there are five more caves. From north to south they are **Hilbert Cave**, the best-decorated cave in the park, a 55-foot crawlway on two levels; **Twin Cave**, a 50-foot passage in talus; **Canoe Cave**, a 35-foot crawlway; **Mallory Cave**, a 42-foot crawlway; and **Storehouse Cave**, a 30-foot walkway of tectonic origin.

Physically fit adults can reach the largest cave in the park, called **Devil's Kitchen**, without a boat if they are willing to wade through waist-deep water. The cave is located on the easily accessible eastern side of the Cedar River, in an area of calm water. From the parking lot, take the Cedar Cliff Trail, which runs past Silurian-age mounds of fossil sea-lily debris. As I hiked toward the cave along this forest trail at dusk, a thunderstorm began to brew. The wind blowing through the gnarled old cedars among the Swiss-cheese rock and the quaint little stone bridges spanning the streams gave the whole place a

Hansel and Gretel atmosphere.

The trail leads up to the top of Cedar Cliff, where there is a stone pavilion or gazebo with a compass rose in its floor. Based on tree-ring studies, it was determined that one of the cedar trees here sprouted in 1527! A row of seven Indian burial mounds is located just up the road from the gazebo. Devil's Kitchen is located in the cliff below the pavilion, but you can't see it from there, nor can you reach it by climbing down the sheer rock face. Instead, turn off the trail before it gets to the top of Cedar Cliff and walk down to the riverbank. Enter the river where the cliff begins; the entrance to the cave is just around the corner. Walk slowly and be careful not to bang your knees against submerged boulders. At the cave, the rock has been worn smooth by the many people who have climbed up to the entrance, which is situated about a dozen feet above the water. The cave, its walls studded with fossils, consists of 150 feet of walking and crawling passages, and is large enough to hold thirty people. About three hundred feet farther upriver along the same shore, and much easier to get into, is **Spider Cave**. It's basically a rockshelter with a large boulder in the center, leaving a crawlway around the perimeter.

Palisades-Dows State Preserve, which is contiguous with Palisades-Kepler State Park, contains **Minott's Cave**, where James Minott set up housekeeping in the late 1860s. However, Minott wasn't the first person to live in the cramped, eight-by-eight-foot cave. When the floor was excavated in 1942 by Charles Reuben Keyes (1871–1951), the father of Iowa archeology, more than 11,000 prehistoric artifacts were recovered. This and surrounding caves are among the best Woodland Indian period sites in Iowa. **The Linn County History Center** in Cedar Rapids features a Minott's Cave diorama, including artifacts found during the excavations. A Minott's Cave exhibit, along with a Palisades-Kepler diorama, can also be seen at the **MacBride Hall Museum** at the University of Iowa in Iowa City.

Directions:	About 3.5 miles west of Mount Vernon off U.S. Highway 30.
Season/hours:	Daily, 4:00 a.m. to 10:30 p.m. Free.
Length:	Various.
Precautions:	Jacket, gloves, and lights. A boat is required to reach most of the caves.
Amenities:	Picnic tables, pavilions, lodge, campground, hiking trails.
Contact:	Palisades-Kepler State Park, RR 2, Mount Vernon, IA 52314. Phone: (319) 895-6039. Web site: www.state.ia.us/parks

Three Bridges Park Caves
Marshall County

BURNIE BEANE (1879–1966) was one of Iowa's greatest fossil collectors. A farmer with no formal training in paleontology, Beane spent countless hours searching the limestone quarries near his hometown of Le Grand for sea lilies and starfish. While it's quite common to find crinoid debris—disarticulated pieces of the stems of the extinct, flowerlike animals known as sea lilies—it is far more rare to come across intact sea lilies in "nests," as Beane did. Sea lilies grew in submarine meadows in the warm, shallow seas of the Mississippian Period (345 to 310 million years ago). Slabs of sea lilies and starfish prepared by Beane can be seen in major museums around the world. The quarry in what is now Three Bridges Park was among his favorite hunting grounds. You can hunt there for caves!

Three Bridges Park, comprising 12 acres of the abandoned limestone quarry, was established in 1960 as one link in a chain of parks forming the Iowa River Greenbelt. Several large, conical mounds of quarry debris, now overgrown with trees, dot the landscape. A half-mile interpretive loop with numbered posts has been constructed along the crest of the limestone ridge, which is crowned by a grove of aspen trees. A swing bridge crosses a gap in the ridge.

The three caves in Three Bridges Park, all located in the former quarry, were mapped by Iowa cavers in 1997. If you look at the quarry face, you will see a zone of small voids in the limestone, dissolved out by groundwater, about halfway up, which marks the level at which you will also find the caves. The largest of the caves is reached by an easy uphill trail from the lower picnic area near the boat ramp. The cave is 12 feet wide with a cone of soil at its mouth. The gravel-floored cave is of stooping height, with several rock pillars along the back wall. An opening at the rear leads to a dark sit-up room, for a total length of 15 feet.

At the opposite, south end of the quarry, near interpretive marker No. 18, is a pair of smaller caves that require a little scrambling to get to. The one on the left is a rock tube 20 feet long with a dry, red mud floor. The walking passage slopes steeply upward into a crawlway; at the end there is a dark sit-up room, the ceiling a boiling mass of crickets. The cave on the right is a rock tube 15 feet long. Notice how

This is the largest of several caves located in a famous fossil quarry at Three Bridges Park near Le Grand.

the walls of both caves are densely covered with crinoid fossils.

The industrial archeology of the park may also be of interest. The wrought-iron Pratt truss bridge over the Iowa River dates back to 1885. It was the third such bridge built in the area, hence the name Three Bridges Park. No longer suitable for vehicular traffic, it serves only pedestrians. A stone-cutting mill is immediately downstream; water was diverted from the river through the mill and then back into the river. A furrow in the ground marks the old raceway.

Directions: From the intersection of U.S. Highway 30 and State Highway 146, west of Le Grand, go one mile west on 30 to Yates Road (gravel). Go two-thirds of a mile north, over the railroad bridge, to Quarry Road (gravel), in the town of Quarry. Go west on Quarry Road one-third of a mile to Three Bridges Road (gravel). Go one-half mile north to where the road ends. A bronze plaque on a boulder marks the location of the park.

Season/hours: Open year round, 4:30 a.m. to 10:00 p.m. Free.

Length: Various.

Precautions: Jacket, gloves, and lights.

Amenities: Picnic tables, restrooms, boat ramp, spearfishing.

Contact: Marshall County Conservation Board, 1302 East Olive, RR 2, Marshalltown, IA 50158. Phone: (641) 754-6303.

26

Wildcat Den State Park
Muscatine County

D EEP IN THE WOODS of Wildcat Den State Park, a simple, arrow-shaped sign marked "Dens" points to a nearby cliff of red sandstone. Now that's an invitation any cave-craving visitor can't pass up! Follow that "advice" and hike to the cliff. There, you'll find a plaque affixed to the outcrop below Wildcat Den, the larger of the park's two dens. The inscription reads, "In memory of Emma C. Brandt and Clara L. Brandt, lovers of nature who donated the original lands in Wildcat Den State Park."

Climb the well-worn rock steps along the face of the outcrop to reach **Wildcat Den** proper, a rockshelter 30 feet across with plenty of room inside and a great view. At the back end, the den pinches down to a crawlway, where you'll encounter a squadron of crane flies hovering in the drafts of cool air that pour from the back of the cave. The crawlway, which is not recommended because of broken beer bottles, leads to a small room where you can barely turn around.

After visiting the big den, try the smaller one—**Bobcat Den**, a hundred feet to the north, which has charms of its own. Bobcat Den's entrance is five feet high, so adults will need to stoop a bit. Like the other den, it pinches down to a tight crawlway at the back end—with more crane flies. The total length is 20 feet.

By hiking the trails in the park you'll encounter other interesting geologic features. Notice, for example, the ubiquitous cross-bedding in the Cherokee sandstone. Cross-bedding, which runs obliquely to the horizontal layering, records stream ripples from when the original sediments that form the rock were being laid down. This coarse-textured reddish sandstone is Pennsylvanian, the same age as Iowa's coal beds. An ancient river that meandered through the coal swamps laid down the sandstone. From studies of the petrified current patterns, it has been determined that the river here flowed to the southwest during the Coal Age. Weathering along the boundaries between these multistoried sand bodies gave rise to the park's dens.

For more of the park's geologic wonders, follow the signs to **Steamboat Rock**, a steamboat-sized slice of bluff, 40 feet high, which broke loose from the parent cliff and slid downslope on the under-

The author rests from his battles with the crane flies at Bobcat Den in Wildcat Den State Park. Photo by Cindy Doty.

lying shale layer. The gap between the two walls is called **Devil's Lane**. A second, narrower passage, branching off from the lane, is known as the Fat Man's Squeeze.

You will find more "steamboat" rocks along the hiking trail. As they broke loose and slid down, the blocks rotated slightly, and some of them have trees growing vertically from the tilted base, which makes for interesting photos. Along the steamboat trail you will also see reddish iron springs that discharge water from the top of the same shale layer that provided lubrication for the sliding "steamboats." Where the groundwater meets the open air, the iron in the water oxidizes and precipitates on the outcrop, forming the rust-colored deposit.

Follow the trail up through the deep, narrow, mossy glen containing the small, unnamed stream tributary of Pine Creek, over a series of wooden footbridges, and past "Horseshoe Bend." The sides of the glen are undercut by deep meander notches, carved by the stream as it washed against either wall. Farther up the glen you will come to the most spectacular overhang of them all, the **Devil's Punchbowl**, a dry waterfall with dark, cavelike voids underneath. A boardwalk leads to an overlook above the bowl. At the very head of the glen you will find a prominent coat of arms carved in the cliff with the date, August 15, 1890. The serif-style lettering and the thick growth of lichen covering it are clues that this is a genuinely old inscription. Other graffiti, dating back to 1861, have been found in the glen.

For those interested in industrial archeology, the **Pine Creek Grist Mill** is an important feature of Wildcat Den State Park. The mill, now on the National Register of Historic Places, was built in 1848 by Benjamin Nye, the earliest white settler in Muscatine County.

Directions: From Muscatine, take State Highway 22 east for 12 miles and watch for the turnoff to the park.

Season/hours: Daily, 4:00 a.m. to 10:30 p.m. Free.

Length: Various.

Precautions: Jacket, gloves, and lights. Climbing up to Wildcat Den could be challenging for some, but Bobcat Den is easily accessible to all.

Amenities: Picnic tables, water faucets, campground.

Contact: Wildcat Den State Park, RR 3, Box 170, Muscatine, IA 52761. Phone: (563) 623-4337. Web site: www.state.ia.us/parks

27

Coldwater Spring State Preserve
Winneshiek County

IT SHOULD BE noted from the outset that Coldwater Cave is accessible only to experienced members of recognized cave clubs. Otherwise, it's the largest and most scenic cave in Iowa and would make a spectacular destination for anyone interested in the state's underground treasures. Because of its significance, however, a brief sketch of the cave here will help people experience it vicariously. Also, nearby Coldwater Spring can be visited. In fact, divers discovered the cave in 1967 by exploring this spring.

Coldwater Spring is found at the base of a 150-foot cliff of Galena limestone along Coldwater Creek, a tributary of the Upper Iowa River. Over time, the spring has carved its way into the cliff, creating a picturesque, sun-dappled alcove festooned with lianas and columbine. Water surges at 8,700 gallons per minute. This is the spot where in the 1850s George Puteney built Cold Spring Mill, a sawmill, when the surrounding land was first settled.

The discovery of Coldwater Cave changed Iowa caving forever. On September 17, 1967, Steve Barnett, a University of Iowa geology student, performed a free dive at Coldwater Spring and swam up into what is now called the First Room. He was acting on a tip from a farmer who claimed that during Prohibition he had set up a still in a room just behind the cliff-face. The room was small, and there was a sump—a place where the ceiling comes down to stream level—at the far end. This second sump, it turned out, was far too long for him to attempt another free dive. Assisted by David Jagnow, Barnett began a series of dives with full scuba gear through a quarter-mile succession of sumps before finally emerging in 1968 into the air-filled main passage that we now call Coldwater Cave. They immediately encountered the first big formation of the cave—a gleaming white stalactite 20 feet long, a good indication of what lay ahead.

Coldwater Cave was found to consist of three miles of magnificent stream gallery intersected by long, narrow side passages that brought in tremendous amounts of water. In the Cascade Passage, for example, these early explorers encountered a series of rimstone dams—natural dams that form mineral deposits, leaving little cascades. In another passage they were puzzled by a banging sound. It

Coldwater Spring is famous as the place where a diver discovered the state's largest cave in 1967.

turned out that it was caused by a pump in a farmer's well that passed down through the cave. On another trip, carrying camping gear, the explorers spent 52 grueling hours in the cave, pushing all the way upstream to the Waterfall Dome. In 1969, Otto Knauth, a newspaper reporter, accompanied the cavers on one of the trips, and his article announced the hitherto secret Coldwater Cave to an unsuspecting world. An underwater gate was installed at the natural spring entrance the following year.

Coldwater Cave contains by far the largest and most pristine cave formations in Iowa. One segment of the main passage, the Gallery Section, is especially well decorated, containing formations such as Big Bertha, a gigantic stalagmite. Shelves of chocolate-colored flowstone line the walls of much of the main passage. These shelves formed on top of mud banks that were later washed away, leaving them unsupported. The cave walls are black from the coating of iron and manganese oxides.

From 1971 to 1975, the state of Iowa leased the land above Coldwater Cave. A 94-foot steel shaft 30 inches in diameter was drilled about midway along the cave's length to facilitate further study. An aluminum ladder was installed in the shaft and a wooden platform at its bottom. A report was prepared, analyzing whether the cave should be made into a tourist cave, but it was eventually decided that this would be too expensive. At the end of the state lease, ownership of the shaft entrance reverted to the owners of the land above. In 1976 the Coldwater Project began, whereby grottoes (cave clubs) from Iowa and surrounding states got together and began exploring the cave with renewed vigor. These efforts continue to the present day.

All trips require wetsuits, as the water is usually 47 degrees Fahrenheit. Without even descending the shaft, the top of which is enclosed by a shed, cavers can tell what passages will be open for exploration by the water level indicated on a stream gauge. During wet weather, the water level can suddenly rise several feet, so the cavers must remain vigilant. Seasonally high levels of carbon dioxide can leave them gasping for breath. In other places, there are great billows of foam, caused by chemicals from the land above, that cavers occasionally have to claw their way through.

The northern passages of Coldwater Cave have long been the focus of intense exploration efforts: some cavers surmise that they may extend all the way to nearby Minnesota! The big trunk passage here splits up into nasty little rock tubes that lead to soaring domes that shower cold water on cave explorers. The passage north has also been blocked by sumps. Cavers long ago adopted a "face-up approach" to navigating these passages—pressing their noses to the ceiling for hundreds of feet and moving very slowly so as to not make waves, a form of recreation not for the faint of heart. They brought new weapons, such as "torpedoes," to the fray. Other goals of Coldwater exploration have been to find a suspected upper level to the cave and to find a way into a parallel cave system—Coldwater's dark twin—that is thought to exist under a neighboring ridge of land.

A variety of wildlife has been observed in Coldwater Cave. Sculpins and trout have been found in the cave stream, their upstream progress limited only by rimstone dams in the passages. Crayfish and salamanders, washed in from the surface, have also been found. Snake Passage was named not for its meandering shape, but for a dead water snake found there. More unexpectedly, bats have been observed and raccoon tracks have been found, suggesting that more openings exist somewhere.

In 1987, Coldwater Cave was declared a National Natural Landmark. As of this writing, about 16.5 miles of passages have been surveyed, surpassing the length of Mystery Cave in Minnesota, which for many years held the record as the longest cave in the Upper Mississippi Valley. In 2003, John Ackerman, owner and operator of the Cave Farm near Spring Valley, Minnesota, drilled a second access shaft, 180 feet deep, into Coldwater Cave, with plans to install an elevator and aboveground facilities.

Directions: From U.S. Highway 52 at Burr Oak, go west on A18 for three miles to W20. Go south on W20 to Coldwater Creek Road, go west one mile to the gravel parking lot on the north side of the road, park at the six white boulders, walk downhill to Coldwater Creek, cross the footbridge, and follow the tire ruts a half mile to Coldwater Spring.

Season/hours: Daily, 4:00 a.m. to 10:30 p.m. Free.

Length: 10 feet.

Precautions: Lengthy hike, expect to get your feet wet.

Amenities: Hiking, picnicking, trout fishing.

Contact: IDNR, 903 Commerce, Suite #4, Decorah, IA 52101. Phone: (563) 382-4895. Web site: www.state.ia.us/parks For more information about Coldwater Cave, see www.caves.org/project/coldwater

Decorah Ice Cave
Winneshiek County

IN 1932, Ripley's Believe It or Not described the Decorah Ice Cave as the "Cave of Paradox" because ice was found inside the cave during the summer but not in winter.

Located at the foot of the towering scenic bluffs of the Upper Iowa River overlooking downtown Decorah, the cave is named for the ice that covers its walls and floor from March to September each year. It's the largest ice cave in North America east of the Black Hills (not to be confused with the sort of ice cave that forms under a glacier).

Several theories were originally proposed to account for the cave's strange behavior. In 1898, Alois Kovarik, an instructor at the Decorah Institute (now Luther College) finally provided the explanation that is still accepted today. Few American caves have had such an influence on the development of cave meteorology.

The ice forms in a unique way. The cave's interior slopes downward, trapping cold air during the winter, which chills the surrounding rocks to below freezing. The air that chills the rock is in turn warmed by that same rock, escaping upward from the cave through fissures and allowing room for more cold air to enter. The ice begins forming in spring (not winter!) when meltwater seeps down through fissures from the outside and refreezes inside the cave. The ice attains its maximum thickness of 10 inches by June, gradually melting during the summer.

This ice creates a unique habitat. A rare species of springtail—a small, wingless insect about the size of a sesame seed—is found in this cave and nowhere else in Iowa. The insect is a glacial relict, whose distribution would otherwise be confined to far northern latitudes. It arrived in the area during the Great Ice Age and decided to remain in this hospitable icebox setting after the glaciers left.

The cave's single, fairly straight passage, 125 feet long, runs parallel to the Galena limestone bluff. The passage was created when a giant slice of bluff detached from the crest and rotated outward at its base, leaving a cave passage with a triangular cross section. The underlying Decorah shale provided lubrication for this movement. The right wall of the passage is intact rock—part of the original bluff—while the left wall is fractured and inclined, an indication that it has moved.

The Decorah Ice Cave was featured in Ripley's Believe It or Not *as the "Cave of Paradox" for its strange behavior.*

At the base of the stone stairway leading up to the cave, there's a memorial to the man who donated the cave and hillside to the city of Decorah in 1955. A sign at the top of the stairway warns visitors about falling rock and the slipperiness of the cave floor when coated with ice. It also states that minors must be accompanied by adults when entering the cave.

The cave's frost-shattered entrance is 6 feet wide and 15 feet high. Follow the sloping passage down into the cave, bracing yourself against the walls to avoid slipping, if necessary. Halfway through the cave you will come to a giant, three-sided rock pillar. Look up into the

Sand Cave and the Sand Painter

Sand Cave is discussed here separately because, even though it is located in a state park, the trail leading to it is very precipitous, with three hundred feet of vertical relief. Park officials have recently closed the trail and no longer want visitors going to the cave. Its location has been removed from park brochures and signage.

Most people are surprised to learn that the highest bluff along the entire length of the Mississippi River is located in Iowa, at Pikes Peak State Park just south of McGregor. The bluffs there soar five hundred feet above the river. Nestled among the ravines of this park is Sand Cave. Debate continues as to whether Sand Cave is natural, artificial, or a little of both. While in other locations the Ordovician-age Saint Peter Sandstone is almost pure white, at Sand Cave it is filled with wild swirls of reddish iron pigment, technically known as Liesegang bands. The bands result from the oxidation and precipitation of iron from groundwater. Not surprisingly, the steep ravine in which the cave is located is known as Pictured Rocks Glen. Beginning at the top with Bridal Veil Falls, a stream passes over a succession of scenic waterfalls embowered with mosses and ferns.

Because of the colorful rocks, Sand Cave actually seems to glow with rosy light at certain times of day. The entrance to the cave is an asymmetrical arch, 20 feet wide, resembling a cresting wave. The dry, sandy floor has a steep incline. Inside, boulders form natural benches. I once found an elaborately built sand castle inside the cave.

The famous sand bottles of Andrew Clemens (1857–1894) are traditionally associated with Sand Cave. Clemens, a McGregor native, filled glass bottles with colored sand, grain by grain, building up elaborate "sand paintings." Each color was collected separately at Sand Cave and placed in its own bag. No glue was used as the grains were held in place by surrounding grains. What makes this even more astonishing was his use of round-top drug jars, forcing him to "paint" the images upside down! Clemens's masterpiece, a bottle containing a portrait of George Washington on horseback, is on display, along with Clemens's tools, at the State Historical Society in Des Moines.

great fissure above you at this point. The rock layers forming the walls of this fissure resemble boxes stacked high in the shelving of a subterranean warehouse. Roots dangle from the ceiling far above. If you shut your light off, you can see a natural skylight.

Beyond the triangular pillar, the passage is gated with rebar, sealing off the ice chamber proper. An interpretive plaque states, "Visitors are cautioned not to proceed beyond the ice chamber, the lowest portion of the cave. The passage beyond this point becomes very small, difficult to traverse, and surrounded by many loose rocks which are easily dislodged." Since the sign was installed before the gate, the point is moot. The Autograph Room, the remotest part of the cave, contains dates back to 1878. It was rediscovered among the boulders in 1973, having lain undisturbed for many years.

The cave has an upper-level passage above the one that you have just walked through, and you will likely see or hear people crawling along this high shelf during your own visit. But it's not recommended for casual visitors. And it's another good reason to wear a hard hat in this cave—to protect against stones dislodged from above!

The history of the Decorah Ice Cave, along with a map of the cave, can be found on the interpretive plaque next to the picnic table at the gravel turnout along Ice Cave Road. Stanley Scarvie briefly commercialized the cave in 1929. Scarvie's improvements included electric lights, a wooden stairway, planks laid over the icy floor, and a small, bark-covered "cave house," the concrete footings of which are still visible. An observation platform was built on the bluff face. A small zoo contained rattlesnakes, raccoons, and monkeys. As many as 5,000 visitors a year came to see the cave. Several nearby competing show caves—some of them run by Scarvie himself!—led to the demise of the operation in 1941.

Despite the great historic and scientific significance of the Decorah Ice Cave, a more interesting cave in terms of variety and challenge (in my opinion) is **Cave Man's Cave**. It's reached by heading up the steep trail from the interpretive sign for the three-acre preserve. There are three entrances to this cave, but only two of them are safe.

The cave entrance easiest to reach is found by following the trail to its westernmost point, beyond the large blocks of limestone, where you will see an opening sloping down into the hill. You'll have to crawl sideways or on your belly for 20 feet, before emerging into a high fissure. After admiring this chamber, crawl under the slab of rock into another high fissure, this one well lit because the block has pulled away from the bluff enough to create a natural skylight. A bit farther on is the exit, which is of walking size.

Hiking up the trail beyond Cave Man's Cave you'll see The Pits— more cave entrances! One of the pits leads to a small cave, while the other is the third entrance to Cave Man's Cave. The passage leads down to a crevice 30 feet deep, so stay out! Continuing uphill along the trail there are several more cave passages paralleling the bluff. At one point, the Catwalk, you can follow the trail along a thin blade of bluff that has separated enough to leave a deep trench on one side. East of the Catwalk, you pass **Devil's Hole** (a deep fissure) and come to the cedar-crowned Ice Cave Tower. You can descend to the entrance of the Decorah Ice Cave by climbing down around the tower, which isn't very difficult. Be careful not to dislodge loose stones onto people visiting the ice cave—or get hit by them yourself.

Upon leaving the preserve, continue east on Ice Cave Road a short distance and drive the scenic loop through **Palisades Park**.

There are more ice caves, albeit unenterable, in **Phelps Park**, on the south side of Decorah. To see them, follow the Oneota Trail along the south bank of the Upper Iowa River. There is an information kiosk explaining algific caves and algific talus slopes. Cold air pouring from the rocks on north-facing slopes maintains a year-round temperature of 37 to 50 degrees Fahrenheit, which supports several plants and snails not found anywhere else south of Canada. Just east of the marker along the trail there is a series of algific vents in the slopes—but no enterable caves. Each vent has a triangular-shaped moss apron on the slope below it, marking the area influenced by the cold air.

Directions:	From U.S. Highway 52 at Decorah, take the Pole Line Road exit east to College Drive, turn right (south) on College Drive past Luther College, turn left (east) on Quarry Street, which turns into Ice Cave Road. Watch for the cave on the left side.
Season/hours:	Although the cave can be visited year round and Ice Cave Park is open from dawn until dusk, ice is found in the cave only from March through September. Free.
Length:	Decorah Ice Cave is 125 feet long, and Cave Man's Cave is several hundred feet long.
Precautions:	Hard hat, jacket, gloves, and lights. Ice on the floor presents a slip hazard.
Amenities:	Picnic tables, hiking.
Contact:	Decorah Parks and Recreation, 801 Park Drive, Decorah, IA 52101. Phone: (563) 382-4158.

29

Dunning's Spring Park
Winneshiek County

WILLIAM PAINTER, the first white settler in Decorah, erected a gristmill at a spring within the city limits in 1849. The elevated position of the spring in the bluffs, relative to the mill below, provided a good head of water. Spring mills are less susceptible to freezing in winter, loss of power during dry weather, and flooding than are mills erected on ordinary surface streams. The spring, however, took the name of its second owner, Dunning, who purchased the mill in 1851 and ran it until the 1870s, when it became the Decorah Marble Works. The mill was used to cut and polish a faux marble quarried locally. The mill was torn down in 1907, its location marked by a boulder in the picnic area. A wonderfully detailed interpretive sign in the park tells the story of Dunning's Spring, complete with historic photos.

The park, a popular picnic spot jammed with cars on hot summer days, features a black, moss-encrusted waterfall set in a cedar-crowned amphitheater of bone-white Galena limestone. The stream that tumbles over the falls boils up from an impressive spring cave, which is not visible from below the waterfall. A boardwalk, beginning at the parking lot, leads up a flight of stairs to a high overlook at the spring cave, which is about 20 feet long. At the right side of the cave, there is a short, mud-floored walking passage several feet long, which serves as an overflow spring exit. Cold air blows from this opening, suggesting more cave passages beyond.

Groundwater descends through fissures in the Galena limestone until it reaches the impermeable Decorah shale; it is then shed laterally, forming the stream that pours from the spring cave. Some cavers suspect that Dunning's Spring is the outlet for the river in Wonder Cave, a former show cave, located several miles to the north. The spring water deposits calcareous tufa, a porous limestone, at the waterfall. This is the most notable tufa deposit in Iowa.

Another historic cave, located on private property at the entrance to Dunning's Spring Park, is known (somewhat confusingly) as **Dunning's Cave**. In fact, it's a one-hundred-foot-long tunnel carved through tufa—not a natural cave. The garagedoor-like opening, easily

Dunning's Spring in Decorah boils up from a cave and pours over this lovely tufa waterfall, the site where a marble mill once stood.

seen from Ice Cave Road, leads to a passage connecting to the house above. A man named Addicken built a brewery here in 1857, which subsequently became the Klein Brewery. A wooden flume tapped Dunning's Spring, and the water power was used to grind barley for beer. In 1882, when Iowa passed a law prohibiting the manufacture of beer, the brewery became a creamery, and the cave was used for storing the product. A former conservation officer, variously known as the Walnut King or Johnny Walnutseed, later used the tufa cave to store nursery stock. He gained his sobriquet for having planted one million walnut trees around the country. Be sure to also visit the **Decorah Ice Cave,** just down the road a bit.

Directions: From U.S. Highway 52 at Decorah, take Pole Line Road exit east to College Drive, turn right (south) on College Drive, past Luther College, turn left (east) on Quarry Street. The park is reached by a short road on the left.

Season/hours: Daily, daylight hours.

Length: 20 feet.

Precautions: No lights or special gear required.

Amenities: Picnic tables.

Contact: Decorah Parks and Recreation, 801 Park Drive, Decorah, IA 52101. Phone: (563) 382-4158.

Malanaphy Springs
Cave and Waterfall
Winneshiek County

THE UPPER IOWA RIVER is noted for its spring caves—for example, Dunning's Spring in downtown Decorah—but Malanaphy Springs State Preserve gives you the opportunity to visit a spring in a more pristine setting. After parking at the trailhead a few miles northwest of Decorah, go past the gate and hike for one mile through the woods along a dirt road that follows the banks of the river. Bluffs of north-facing Galena limestone appear on your right, and you pass large rock falls, float blocks, and isolated stone towers. At many places there are holes blowing cold air—enough to cause plants to bend over—creating algific talus slopes. At other places the slopes are clothed with Canada yew. Stay off the slopes because they are easily damaged; walking on them shifts the stones, tearing the vegetation and closing the vents.

At the end of the road lies a fire pit, from which you can hear the noisy spring on the slopes above you. Follow the footpath up the slope to **Malanaphy Cave**, whose frost-shattered entrance has an interesting pine tree shape. Notice that the spring doesn't boil up at the rear of the cave, as you might expect, but from around two sides of a boulder near its entrance. On a hot, muggy day the interior of the cave provides delicious relief, complete with convenient ledges to sit on—sort of like a sauna in reverse! The cave is 10 feet high and 20 feet long.

Don't leave without visiting the 10-foot **Malanaphy waterfall**. Follow the stream from the cave down to where it plunges over the falls into the Upper Iowa River. The waterfall is coated with calcareous tufa and moss. A bronze plaque near the falls commemorates Fred Biermann, who purchased this area in 1947 for preservation. From the falls, you can look out over farmland on the north side of the river.

Another, but much smaller spring cave, can be found at the nearby **Falcon Springs Wildlife Area**. From U.S. Highway 52 in Decorah, go 4.7 miles west on Pole Line Road. From the gate, hike one mile north to a stream at the northern tip of the preserve and follow the stream to its source—a small cave at the foot of a 50-foot cliff. If nothing else, it's a nice hike!

Malanaphy Spring pours from a cave and tumbles over a waterfall into the Upper Iowa River, northwest of Decorah.

Directions: From the Luther College exit of U.S. Highway 52 at Decorah, head west on County Road W20 (Pole Line Road) and follow its many twists and turns. W20 turns into Bluffton Road in a few miles. You will see the words "Malanaphy Farm" painted in large letters on the side of a red barn. The preserve is just around the bend from here. Turn at the sign on the right side of the road just before the bridge over the Upper Iowa River and park in the gravel lot.

Season/hours: Daily, 4:00 a.m. to 10:30 p.m. Free.

Length: 20 feet.

Precautions: Bring lights. There is a hike of one mile, and the slope leading up to the spring cave is steep and covered with loose stones.

Amenities: Hiking, canoe access.

Contact: IDNR, 903 Commerce, Suite #4, Decorah, IA 52101. Phone: (563) 382-4895.
Web site: www.state.ia.us/parks

31
Troll Cave
Winneshiek County

G EORGE KNUDSON, professor of chemistry at Luther College in Decorah, was obsessed with trolls—an affliction perhaps natural to the residents of a town steeped in Norwegian heritage. In his 1976 book, Decorah Trails and Trolls, Knudson described Troll Cave in **Twin Springs Park** as follows:

During most of the year no water flows from this large opening. About six feet down, a cave opens up and runs back into the hill about 50 feet and intersects a stream which has its outlet at Twin Springs, across the road. The cave is only about 14 inches high (convenient troll height), but two brave spelunkers crawled into it in 1975. They reported that the cave has a very strong smell of trolls and that they heard many strange noises in the upstream passage which indicated that the trolls had retreated to that point, were very angry, and were planning to release enough water to flood the lower part of the cave. The explorers made a rapid exit and no one has entered since.

My personal exploration of this cave compels me to vouch for some—but not all!—of this description. For one thing, in spite of its angry trolls, the cave has been entered many times since 1976. But the cave should not be attempted unless you are physically fit and willing to get muddy. The entrance is located at the head of a ravine on the opposite side of the road from the springs in Twin Springs Park. You can usually hear water at the entrance. After passing through the slot at the bottom of the overhang—which is admittedly not for everyone—you find yourself in a flat-ceilinged cave passage about two feet high (not 14 inches, as Knudson claimed!) and six feet wide. It would be a very comfortable hands-and-knees crawl were it not for the thick, wet mud bearing the impression of countless raccoon footprints (perhaps mistaken for the footprints of trolls?). After crawling 50 feet you come to a joint in the Galena limestone that contains a stream passage. Do not enter the cold stream passage; it ends within a short distance anyway. Upon leaving the cave, you will be covered with mud, which you can wash off at the springs just across the road.

Twin Springs Creek, which flows through the park, rises from the

This cave in Twin Springs Park, Decorah, is rumored to be inhabited by trolls!

twin, stone-walled basins at Twin Springs, formerly called Union Springs. The Gaston scale factory, which produced platform-weighing scales, was built at Twin Springs in 1880 to take advantage of water power. Later, fish ponds and raceways, the remains of which are still visible, were constructed. The ridge above the springs, called Pine Point, has one of the largest remaining stands of native white pine in Iowa. I love this place for its pine-scented air!

Be sure to visit **Siewers Springs State Hatchery** (pronounced "seevers" by locals) along Trout Run Road. With a flow of 6,000 gallons per minute, the spring was used to power mills in the early days. After heavy rain, the spring gets muddy, so the water is routed into a siltation basin and then aerated and pumped into the trout-rearing tanks. The hatchery is open to the public.

Directions: From U.S. Highway 52 in Decorah, just north of its intersection with State Highway 9, follow the signs to Twin Springs Park. Follow the gravel road to the western end of the park, where the stream emerges from the ground. One-tenth of a mile farther west along the road, on the opposite side, you will see a ditch that is usually dry, follow it until you come to a limestone overhang, at the base of which you will find the cave entrance.

Season/hours: Daily, 4:00 a.m. to 10:30 p.m. Free.

Length: 100 feet.

Precautions: Full caving gear. Hard hat, jacket, gloves, and lights. The cave is not appropriate for children, and the narrow entrance is not for seriously overweight individuals. The cave is wet and muddy. Do not enter in wet weather.

Amenities: Picnic tables.

Contact: Decorah Parks and Recreation, 801 Park Drive, Decorah, IA 52101. Phone: (563) 382-4158.

Section II
Mining
Museums

IOWA'S TWO most significant mining industries have been lead and coal, but its underground has yielded many other minerals over the years. Other metals mined include zinc, found generally where lead was mined; the sedimentary iron ore deposits of Allamakee County; and gold at scattered locations. Industrial minerals were quarried from the Fort Dodge gypsum beds and the Clayton silica mine. Sand and gravel, called aggregate, so much in demand nowadays for construction projects, is obtained along Iowa's major stream valleys. When aggregate is mixed with cement, it forms concrete.

Clay pits have provided drainage tile for drying out the wet prairies—and for sewer pipe, farm silos, and bricks. Oil has also been found, especially in Washington County, but in very limited quantities. Peat, cut from bogs in Iowa's most recently glaciated areas, was once used for fuel, but horticultural purposes now absorb most of the output. Finally, it is interesting to note that perhaps the most unusual "mining rush" to strike Iowa involved freshwater pearls, harvested from clams in the Mississippi River. Numerous factories were established along the river to fashion the shells into decorative buttons. Muscatine, the center of this trade, became known as the Pearl City.

Stone quarrying has also played a significant role in the development of Iowa's industry. Although most stone quarried now is used in crushed form, whether as aggregate, for surfacing roads, or for agricultural lime, dimensional (building) stone was once in great demand. Stone City—later famous as the location of Grant Wood's art colony—was named for its quarries, which provided Anamosa stone for buildings across the country. The Old State Quarry, now a preserve, provided stone for the Old State Capitol in Iowa City. The cement ledges of Mason City, which provided the raw material for Portland cement, played a role in displacing the lime-burning industry of Hurstville. Gilmore City was dubbed the "Limestone Capital of Iowa." The Jasper Pool, a flooded quarry carved into pinkish Sioux Quartzite, is now the centerpiece of Gitchie Manitou State Preserve in the northwest corner of Iowa. The Precambrian-age (older than 600 million years) Sioux Quartzite is the oldest kind of rock quarried in the state. Iowa is also home to a unique quarry ghost town, known as Lithograph City (located northwest of Charles City), which existed around World War I and was eventually plowed under the cornfields.

The most common form of museum exhibit relating to Iowa mining is the mine replica. Indeed, the construction of mine replicas seems to be an industry in its own right in southern Iowa! And whereas the cave maker's material of choice is shotcrete (sprayed concrete), the mine maker's favorite material seems to be plywood—usually painted black. Add a suitably attired mannequin, and you have a mine! Exhibits in museums have been included in this guidebook only if they are permanent exhibits and if they contain more than just a few rusty picks and shovels. ■

Lead Mines

O NE OF THE world's richest lead-bearing regions exists in the tristate area where Iowa, Wisconsin, and Illinois meet. The first American mineral rush began here in the 1820s, with Wisconsin accounting for the lion's share of the lead output. It derived its nickname, the Badger State, from early lead miners who lived in the pits that they dug into hillsides in their search for the mineral.

Galena (lead sulfide) is a heavy, cubic, metallic-gray mineral and a major lead ore. In Galena limestone, galena occurs as veins running east and west (known locally as "ranges") or as cavity linings. Other rock layers also contain lead deposits but in a somewhat different form. Galena and its associated minerals—and almost all of the Iowa minerals can be found in these deposits—are believed to have precipitated from hot brines that seeped through the rocks.

Galena, which has been found in native burial mounds, was obviously known to the inhabitants long before the arrival of Europeans. The ore was probably collected from stream gravel, as loose pieces on the land surface (called "float"), or pried from outcrops with deer antlers. The journals of the early Jesuit explorers mention the rich lead deposits of the Mississippi Valley.

In addition to the ornamental use of galena by Native Americans, the arrival of French fur traders in the seventeenth century, who needed lead for their firearms, created a strong demand for the mineral and provided the natives with additional incentive for mining lead. Reportedly, Iowa was a major source of lead during the American Revolution.

In 1788, Julien Dubuque, a French-Canadian trader, having obtained a valuable mining concession from the Meskwaki (Fox) Indians, began mining lead near the present-day city bearing his name. The endeavor was centered at Catfish Creek, the site of an Indian village. Despite the native concession, Dubuque took the additional step of asking Spain to recognize his claim. Spain had acquired all the land west of the Mississippi from France in 1763. This land grant, which he dubbed the "Mines of Spain," was 21 miles long and 9 miles wide, fronting the Mississippi River from where the Little Maquoketa River entered on the north to Tete Des Morts Creek on the south, including what is now the city of Dubuque. The present Mines of Spain Recreation Area, dedicated in 1981, is located south of the city and comprises about 1 percent of this original Spanish land grant. The Julien Dubuque Monument, on the bluff above Catfish Creek, was constructed in 1897.

Henry Schoolcraft, who later achieved fame as the discoverer of the source of the Mississippi River, visited the Dubuque lead mines in 1820 and documented the native mining techniques. Women and old men performed the work. Shallow trenches and drifts were dug with picks and shovels, but no underground shafts were dug. Loose ore was collected, and when solid bedrock was encountered, it was shattered by "fire setting," which involved heating the rock and dousing it with water. Archeological surveys of the Mines of Spain in the 1980s revealed the location of several hundred mining sites from this period.

Although the Louisiana Purchase of 1803 included the Mines of Spain, the Native American title to the land was not extinguished until the Black Hawk Purchase of 1832, after which white miners and settlers flooded the area. Lead mining now went underground with a vengeance. Using black powder and shafts, the depth of the mines was limited only by the water table. In 1835, the Scotch Hearth, a blast furnace that smelted lead ore into "pigs" weighing about 72 pounds each, was introduced. (Before this, the Native American method of smelting had produced "plats," or slabs.) By the 1840s, surface mining was a thing of the past. A contemporary description of the Langworthy lode provides a feeling for what it was like inside an early Dubuque lead mine:

They began to examine the cave for minerals, each man carrying a lamp or candle. Passing along through various windings and narrow spaces they suddenly came to one of the subterranean vaults which was completely filled with the shining ore, lighted up and sparkling like diamonds, or lying in great masses or adhering to the sides and roof of the cave in huge cubes.

Iowa's lead production peaked in the 1840s. The California Gold Rush of 1849 left the lead mines all but deserted, and it took many years for the industry to recover. Beginning in 1880, a second wave of mining, this time for zinc, which was actually more abundant than lead, swept the area. Abandoned lead mines were reopened and worked for zinc ore, which had been left untouched the first time around. Smithsonite (zinc carbonate), or "drybone," was mined, and later, sphalerite (zinc sulfide), or "blackjack," was recovered from below the water table. The last zinc mine near Dubuque closed in 1910, although there was a brief attempt to revive the industry in the early 1950s. After that, the Iowa Grotto (the local branch of the National Speleological Society) undertook the exploration and mapping of the abandoned lead mines, which required a great deal of ascending and descending by way of ropes. New climbing devices were invented in the process. As many as 2,000 mine shafts underlie Dubuque, some of which sometimes suddenly rise to the surface. Bat studies have also been conducted in the mines.

To commemorate Iowa's oldest industry, a lead smelter and a pile of lead ingots were incorporated into the state seal. ■

Lead Crevice
Dubuque County

3 2

D URING MY COLLEGE years I spent some time crawling through the storm sewers of Dubuque—usually late at night!—trying to enter abandoned lead mines that honeycomb the city. I actually got into one called the Level Crevice mine. Fortunately, you won't have to undergo such an ordeal when you visit this part of Iowa. A lead crevice has been recreated at the **National Mississippi River Museum and Aquarium** in Dubuque, operated by the Dubuque County Historical Society.

The museum complex, where you can easily spend the whole day, is housed in two adjoining buildings, but the lead crevice is located in the **Fred W. Woodward Riverboat Museum**. At the entrance to this museum you are invited to "Noodle a Catfish"—a low-tech fishing method in which fishermen stick their hands into dark, underwater holes, hoping that catfish will bite down, so they can pull them out. Fishermen sometimes drowned performing this operation if the catfish happened to be too big! The museum's catfish is mechanical, however, with a convenient above-water hole and a gentle bite.

A short video clip at the entrance to the lead crevice describes the history of lead mining in Dubuque. A windlass (hoist) on top of the crevice, cranked by an ersatz shirtless miner, shows how lead ore was hoisted from the mines through shafts. A sign over the crevice warns, "Enter at Your Own Risk," but there's nothing remotely dangerous inside. The winding crevice, illuminated by imitation candles, is 4 feet high, 2 feet wide, and 20 feet long, so adults will need to stoop while walking through it. The exhibit would have improved if the walls had been encrusted with simulated cavity linings of galena cubes to mimic the real lead crevices under Dubuque (see the description of the Langworthy lode in the introduction to this section).

The Lead Rush exhibit, in the same room as the lead crevice, showcases "the first major American mineral rush." A lead ladle and various sizes of lead shot, together with a three-foot-high model of the Old Shot Tower, are on display. Pigs (ingots) of lead are stacked up on the floor. A glass case contains mining tools, and a large, silvery chunk of galena (lead sulfide) is available for you to touch. An oil painting, "Julien

The Clayton Silica Mine

The Saint Peter Sandstone, a 99 percent pure quartz sand, is in high demand for certain industrial uses. This sandstone has been heavily mined at Crystal City, Missouri; Ottawa, Illinois; Saint Paul, Minnesota; and other locations, including Iowa.

The largest silica-producing operation in Iowa was located at Clayton on the Mississippi River. From 1878 to 1929, sandstone was quarried from the river bluffs and sold to glass companies and foundries. A second quarry, which supplied materials for a brick and tile plant, operated during the 1920s. Clayton's third, and largest, operation was run by the Langworthy Silica Company, which began quarrying in 1916. It supplied foundry sand to the John Deere Tractor Works.

By 1945, it was apparent that the removal of the overlying soil and rock at this third quarry was too expensive, so underground mining began on the room-and-pillar plan, whereby rooms were excavated and pillars of unmined rock were left to support the ceiling. The dimensions of a typical room measured 40 feet square and 50 feet high. The Martin-Marietta Corporation, a leader in aerospace as well as aggregates, operated the mine from 1959 until 1982, when mining ceased. Since then, the enormous mine, with 14 miles of passages underlying 60 acres, has been used for underground storage, mostly of corn but also including cottonseed, fishmeal, fertilizer, logs, coal, and tires. If you drive to the south end of Clayton, you will see the access road to the mine. The road runs along the foot of the river bluff but is marked "Private Road—No Trespassing." It's often busy with grain trucks.

The Clayton silica mine has been used for other purposes. During the Cold War it was designated as a civil defense shelter capable of housing 44,000 people—more than twice the population of Clayton County. The mine was stocked with food, water, and medical supplies. The mine also serves as a bat hibernaculum.

Dubuque and the Mesquakie Indians," commemorates the fateful moment in 1788 when he received his valuable mining concession.

The Riverboat Museum also contains a cutaway model of the steamboat Dubuque and artifacts from the famous Diamond Jo steamboat line. A model of a "U.S. Snag Boat" shows the split hull design that facilitated the removal of giant trees from the river. Try out your balance on the "floating" log raft, which, by the clever use of mirrors, seems to extend for acres in all directions, just like the real thing. A model of the Dubuque Ice Harbor fills an entire room. It includes the Dubuque Boat & Boiler Works—"the largest inland waters shipbuilder in the United States"—and other industries that once lined the Ice Harbor. The Army Corps of Engineers constructed ice harbors as winter refuges for riverboats.

The "Clamming on the Mississippi" exhibit features a full-size johnboat occupied by a mannequin that is using a crowfoot dredge, a nasty device that devastated clam populations along the river when it was introduced in the 1890s. Dredge lines were pulled along the bottom of the river, and the clams, feeling the hooks, snapped shut, inadvertently snagging themselves. Clams were harvested for pearls and their shells were made into buttons.

A display of different kinds of clams, "From River Bottom to Shirt Front," further explains this industry. Never have such colorful names been given to such basically drab creatures. Examples of some of the monikers, based predominantly on the clam's shape, are Butterfly, Elephant's Ear, Fawnfoot, Lady Finger, Monkey Face, Pancake, Pig Toe, Pink Heelsplitter, Pocketbook, Sheep's Nose, Snuffbox, Spectacle Case, Strawberry, Warty Back, Washboard, and so on! In the late nineteenth and early twentieth centuries, the heyday of Iowa's button industry, Muscatine (located downriver from Dubuque) became known as Pearl City or the Pearl Button Capital of the World. Soon afterward, the industry was hit with competition from cheaper plastic buttons and languished.

Finally, examine some cabinets of curios from the original Richard Herrmann Museum of Natural History, established in the 1870s, which became the nucleus of the present museum.

The William Woodward Discovery Center, right next door, features five large freshwater aquariums filled with prehistoric-looking Mississippi River fishes. Take a trip down the river in the wide-screen Journey Theater, with its surround sound, which even recreates realistic vibrations from the New Madrid earthquake of 1811-1812. (The New Madrid earthquake was one of the most powerful earthquakes to strike North America in historical times, causing the Mississippi River to flow backwards at one point! It was named after the town of New Madrid, Missouri.) Try out your navigational skills in the virtual pilothouse of a towboat. There are several other hands-on activities, including the River Wetlab, with its aquatic critters, and a stream table for experimenting with river dynamics. Just outside are the Woodward Wetlands, where you can explore the natural habitat of the Mississippi along a boardwalk trail.

The National Rivers Hall of Fame, on the upper level of the Discovery Center, features biographies of famous river people from all across America, from explorers, such as Lewis and Clark, to builders of boats and bridges, famous riverboat captains, and artists, writers, and musicians whose works have been inspired by the river.

A museum ticket also entitles you to a self-guided tour of the *William M. Black*, a steamboat accorded National Historic Landmark status, moored in the Ice Harbor. Nearly the size of a football field, this 1934 suction dredge was used to maintain a navigable channel in the Missouri River, making it possible to use the river for shipping during World War II. You can make arrangements to sleep overnight on the "boat and breakfast." The boatyard here features the Logsdon Sand & Gravel Company boat, and several others.

Your museum ticket is also good for discount admission to the **Mathias Ham House**, near scenic Eagle Point Park on the north side of Dubuque. This 1856 Victorian house (reportedly haunted!) was built for Ham, the first major American lead miner to follow in Julien Dubuque's footsteps. It's open for tours by costumed interpreters and includes a 10-minute orientation film, Lead Rush. A restored 1833 lead miner's log cabin—said to be Iowa's oldest building—is located on the grounds.

You can also visit (but not enter) the **Old Shot Tower** on the Dubuque waterfront, near the museum. The tower, a 150-foot obelisk, was constructed in 1856 of limestone with a brick top. Workers ascended ladders to a furnace at the top where they poured molten lead through sieves. As the molten droplets fell they formed round lead shot before splashing into a tub of water at the bottom of the tower. The shot was then polished in a rotating cask.

The tower produced shot for the Union Army during the Civil War. Within a few years the tower was purchased by a rival manufacturer in St. Louis, who promptly shut it down. Local shot making continued underground, in the abandoned mine shafts of Dubuque. The tower was later used by a lumber company as a fire observation tower. It became involved in a conflagration itself, however, appearing from a distance as "a great pillar of flame, out of which shot masses of sparks, resembling those shot out of a Roman candle," according to one eyewitness. Luckily, it survived.

Directions: From downtown Dubuque, turn east onto Third Street, follow the signs to the Ice Harbor.

Season/hours: Daily, 10:00 a.m. to 6:00 p.m. Closed Thanksgiving and Christmas. Fee.

Precautions: None.

Amenities: Museum Store, Depot Café, William M. Black Boat and Breakfast; Grand Harbor Resort and Waterpark is nearby.

Contact: National Mississippi River Museum and Aquarium, 350 East 3rd Street, Dubuque, IA 52001. Phone: (800) 226-3369. Web site: www.rivermuseum.com

33
Mines of Spain Recreation Area
Dubuque County

THE E. B. LYONS Interpretive Center, headquarters for the Mines of Spain Recreation Area located a few miles south of Dubuque, contains an impressive lead-mining exhibit. Prize specimens of lead ore and artifacts from the vicinity—such as old mining tools and the remains of ore cars—are on display. Photos of the many abandoned lead mines honeycombing the Mines of Spain area cover the walls. The Junkermann Farm display rounds out the exhibit. Otto Junkermann, the first wholesale druggist west of the Mississippi River, purchased this land in 1859 and built many of the structures seen along the hiking trails.

The Mines of Spain Recreation Area, a National Historic Landmark, covers more than two square miles. Before embarking on your exploration of this rugged landscape, study the tabletop relief model in the interpretive center to better orient yourself. Starting near

A rail fence surrounds a collapsed mineshaft on the Lead Mine Trail in the Mines of Spain Recreation Area.

the center, follow the **Lead Mine Trail**—part of the Junkermann Trail—a gravel path along which are several subterranean features. You come first to a sinkhole resulting from a collapsed mineshaft—similar to the sinkholes that sometimes appear suddenly in the streets of downtown Dubuque when mines collapse. Surrounded by a rail fence, the pit has a tree growing out of it. The accompanying historical plaque describes shaft mining and smelting. The all-important Scotch Hearth, which made lead smelting far easier, is described. A little farther on there are more pits, but these originated from pit mining, which predates shaft mining. Indeed, the hills south of Dubuque are pockmarked with hundreds of these pits, dug in the restless pursuit of lead ore, leaving the area as if it had been carpet bombed. Pits yielding nothing were called "sucker holes."

The Lead Mine Trail winds downhill through the woods to a meadow and the base of a rocky outcrop where there are miscellaneous farm outbuildings. **The Wine Cellar** in the side of the hill, later converted into a religious grotto, is large enough for several people to stand in. Junkermann grew grapes and made wine on this farm. The **Root Cellar**, built against natural rock chimneys and clothed with mosses and ferns, has a mysterious appearance. Stooping to pass through the small door of this damp, dark stone cellar, with its barrel-vaulted masonry roof and brick floor, is like entering a gloomy dungeon. The cellar initially served for refrigeration and later as a smokehouse. More stone foundations from the Junkermann farm are found along the trail, but none of them have subterranean associations.

At this point, you can either return to your vehicle at the interpretive center and drive into the Mines of Spain proper or hike the one-mile Mesquakie Trail, which branches off here and connects to **Catfish Creek State Preserve**—the birthplace of lead mining in Iowa—which occupies the northern half of the Mines of Spain area. In this preserve you will find the site of the village where the lead-mining Mesquakie Indians lived. Ironically, this area also contains the Fessler Mine, the last lead mine in the area to close, in 1914. It's off-limits to the public.

Explore the nearby **Horseshoe Bluff Quarry**, carved in the center of a hill. From the quarry parking lot, look for the trail heading south; follow it around the hill to where it enters the quarry. This spectacular canyonlike quarry shaped like a horseshoe has soaring walls of Galena dolomite crowned with cedars. An interpretive trail winds through the scrub, with several stops where visitors can learn about calcite, chert, lead, and the geology of the quarry itself. Scanning the walls of the quarry, you can see a massive, buff-colored layer of rock (the Wise Lake Formation) overlying a drab, cherty, thinly bedded layer (the Dunleith Formation). The floor of the quarry, which appears to be a blacktop surface, is actually a blackened pyritic hardground. (A hard-ground represents a hiatus in sediment deposition that occurred during the period that rock was being laid down in an ancient sea; the blackening is caused by pyrite, an iron mineral.)

The quarry is also a great bird-watching spot. Midway through the quarry there are benches where you can sit and watch a cliff riddled with the nesting holes of swallows. Limestone quarries are veritable aviaries because the many chinks in the rock provide good nesting spots.

Back at the quarry parking lot again, follow the trail north this time and you will come to a quarry overlook with a spectacular two-way vista. To the north you have a wonderful view of the city of Dubuque. To the south—framed by the walls of the quarry—you will see Nine Mile Island in the Mississippi River. A plaque at the quarry overlook describes the Galena Group dolomites and the story of the quarry. It also explains "stream piracy," for which the Mines of Spain is noted. This phenomenon occurs when the upstream portion of one stream is captured ("pirated") by the head-ward growth of another stream, thus diverting the water.

Be sure to visit the **Julien Dubuque Monument**, the most widely recognized landmark at the Mines of Spain, located atop a 170-foot bluff. The 28-foot-high stone tower was built in 1897, and from here you have a scenic vista of the Mississippi River valley. At the base of the bluff is Catfish Cave, described in Section I.

Directions: From U.S. Highway 52, two miles south of Dubuque and one mile south of its intersection with U.S. Highway 61, turn east onto Old Massey Road and follow the signs. The E. B. Lyons Interpretive Center is located on Old Bellevue Road, which intersects U.S. Highway 52 immediately south of U.S. Highway 61.

Season/hours: The recreation area is open daily, 4:00 a.m. to 10:30 p.m. Free. The E. B. Lyons Interpretive Center is open Monday through Friday from 9:00 a.m. to 4:00 p.m. year round; weekends, 12:00 to 4:00 p.m. from April 15 to October 15. Free.

Precautions: Because the Mines of Spain is also a wildlife man-agement area, wear blaze orange during hunting season. The Horseshoe Quarry is closed from late winter to early spring due to falling rock.

Amenities: Hiking, picnicking.

Contact: E. B. Lyons Interpretive Center, 8999 Bellevue Heights, Dubuque, IA 52003.
Phone: (563) 556-0620.
Web site: www.state.ia.us/parks

Coal Mines

THE PENNSYLVANIAN PERIOD, also called the Coal Age, was named for rock exposures in the area now occupied by the state of Pennsylvania that date from 310 million to 280 million years ago. Pennsylvanian-age rocks form the uppermost bedrock layer for more than one-third of Iowa. The swamps that contributed the plant matter that eventually became coal flourished in the region's river deltas and low-lying coastlines. While more than 3,000 fossil plant species have been found in coal deposits, its best-known coal plants are the great lepidodendrons—often labeled "coal palm trees" in Iowa museums—that grew to a height of more than one hundred feet. The fossilized "bark" of these trees, with its diamond-shaped patterning, is often mistaken for petrified snakeskin. The best local diorama of a Pennsylvanian coal swamp can be seen in MacBride Hall at the University of Iowa in Iowa City.

Iowa's coal seams are small compared with those elsewhere. The Mystic Seam, one of Iowa's largest, underlies 1,500 square miles—just a bit larger than most Iowa counties—and averages only 2.5 feet thick. In any given coal-mining area, however, there was usually a "first" (uppermost) and "second" seam and often a "third" seam below that. Iowa coal towns could go through boom and bust cycles based on the discovery and mining of successively deeper seams.

Low-rank coals, such as lignite, flame easily but have low heating power. High-rank coals, such as anthracite, are difficult to ignite. Iowa's coal falls somewhere in between, in the bituminous range. Iowa coal is good for heating and steam making but not for coking and gas making. Historically speaking, there was a widespread prejudice against switching from wood to coal for home heating, due to its sootiness, but on the treeless prairies of Iowa, people were grateful to have coal.

French explorers first reported coal in Iowa based on exposures along the Des Moines River in 1721. Lieutenant Albert Lea, sent to investigate the Black Hawk Purchase in 1835, also reported coal out-crops along that river. Five years later, the state's first coal mine was opened by Samuel Knight in Van Buren County. The first geological survey to systematically examine Iowa coal deposits was led by David Dale Owen, who published his report in 1852.

Before the Civil War, much of Iowa's coal was used by steamboats plying the Des Moines River. After that war, railroads became the chief consumer—and a major factor in the expansion of the western frontier. Abraham Lincoln chose Council Bluffs, at the western end of the state, to be the eastern terminus for the transcontinental railroad. Iowa was the last coaling stop for westbound trains until Colorado was reached. For a time, Iowa was the leading coal-producing state west of the Mississippi.

The demand for Iowa coal was either seasonal or constant. Mines supplying local heating needs operated only during the fall and winter months, leaving their miners seasonally unemployed unless they also farmed. This seasonality led to the miner being regarded as a sort of migrant worker, a factor that delayed unionization in Iowa.

Iowa railroads, on the other hand, created a year-round demand for coal. Railroad mines provided more stability and a higher stan-dard of living for their workers. These so-called "captive mines" were often railroad subsidiaries. For example, the Chicago & North Western Railroad owned the Consolidation Coal Company, whose No. 18 coal mine became the largest in Iowa.

The isolated locations of many Iowa railroad mines, far from existing settlements, led to the construction of company towns. Miners in these locales labored under a paternalistic system con-trolled by mine owners who vigorously resisted any attempts at unionization. Any dissent on the part of the miners resulted in dis-missal. And miners were very easily replaced, often by new immi-grants.

Iowa company towns usually consisted of rows of wooden houses and a company store. Houses were intentionally made cheap because it was understood that Iowa coal seams didn't last very long. The average life span of an Iowa coal mine was ten years—about half that of a mine in the eastern United States. Unless incorporated, a com-pany town frequently became a ghost town when the local mines shut down. Buxton is the largest and best-known example of an Iowa company town that met such a fate.

The period from 1895 to 1925 was the most productive for Iowa coal mining. The peak year was 1917, when Iowa ranked fifth in the nation, with nine million tons of coal being produced from 450 mines worked by 18,000 miners. Overall, there have been 6,000 underground mines in 38 of Iowa's 99 counties. Monroe County has the distinction of being the all-time leading coal-producing county in Iowa, followed by Polk County. The string of counties along the Des Moines River has always been the heart of Iowa coal country.

Iowa's coal mining methods, like those elsewhere in the country, took several forms. The earliest and most primitive technique was based on the discovery of coal in outcrops along stream banks. Digging coal from these outcrops, following the seam inward, led to the simplest kind of mine, called a drift. A more involved kind of mine was the slope mine, in which a sloping tunnel, called an adit, was dug to access the coal seam. As mining equipment improved over the years, vertical shaft mines became more common, even though no Iowa coal mines were more than a few hundred feet deep. In the 1940s there was a shift from underground mining to surface mining, a technique in which ordinary earth-moving equipment was used to strip away the overburden and remove the coal. Surface mining created an economy of scale. Compare the capacity of a large dump truck that can easily maneuver above ground to that of a small, wooden coal car that has to be transported to the surface, and you get the picture.

Coal mines in Iowa adopted one of two basic underground layouts, room-and-pillar and longwall. The room-and-pillar mine made extensive use of blasting to excavate long, tunnel-like rooms. Little supportive timbering was required because pillars of coal were left in place to support the roof. The pillars represented perhaps half the coal in the seam, however, so in many cases the pillars were later "robbed," or mined away, when that part of the mine was abandoned. The subsequent collapse of the mine often resulted in the appearance of sinkholes at the surface.

In the longwall method, all the coal was removed, so extensive timbering was required to support the roof. No blasting was involved. Instead, the coal face was undercut by removing the clay from under the coal seam. At first this was done with a hand pick, later with coal cutters that resembled giant chain saws. The weight of the overburden pressing down caused the unsupported wedge of coal to fall into the undercut. Waste material, called packwall, was used to backfill mined-out areas.

Since 1900 more than one hundred thousand workers have been killed in U.S. coal mines. The most common cause of death in Iowa mines was collapsing roof slates, which usually occurred when a longwall miner dislodged a supporting prop. On the other hand, the worst single mining accident in Iowa history, the Lost Creek disaster of 1902, occurred when 20 men were killed in an explosion in a room-and-pillar mine. Deadly explosions like this eventually led to the appointment of certified shot (blast) examiners, who went through the mine double-checking the miner's placement of the explosives.

And blasting at the end of the shift, after the miners had left the mine, replaced random blasting.

Iowa's coal industry declined for economic reasons, not because of resource depletion; only 5 percent of Iowa's coal has been removed. Important factors in the industry's decline include the shift from coal to diesel fuel by the railroads in the 1940s, the shift from coal to fuel oil or natural gas for home heating, and the passage of the Clean Air Act of 1970, which placed stringent controls on sulfur dioxide emissions. To meet air-quality standards, Iowa's high-sulfur coal could be washed to remove the sulfur or blended with low-sulfur coal from other sources, but the extra processing makes the coal less competitive. The last underground coal mine in Iowa shut down in 1981 and the last surface mine in 1994. But the scars left by coal mining can still be seen on the landscape. ■

34

Appanoose County Historical and Coal Mining Museum
Appanoose County

A CCORDING TO ONE local account, coal in Appanoose County was discovered by Mormons traveling from Illinois to Utah in the winter of 1846. They dug fire pits and, in the process, uncovered coal lying conveniently near the surface. The Mormons named this area in far southern Iowa Sharon, after the hills of Palestine. In nearby Sharon Bluffs State Park, deep ruts from their carts, preserved over many years, can still be seen.

The coal wealth of Appanoose County was based on the 30-inch Mystic Seam, whose minable extent was more than 1,500 square miles, one of the largest seams in Iowa. The Appanoose County Historical and Coal Mining Museum in Centerville is housed in the 1903 post office and contains a historic post office display on the first floor. Over the entrance to the basement, a sign points you to the Coal Mining Museum, which provides two different simulated underground experiences in separate rooms.

The first thing to do at the museum is view The Last Pony Mine, a classic 23-minute documentary about coal mining in Iowa. It was filmed at the New Gladstone Mine, eight miles west of Centerville, reportedly the last mine in the United States to use ponies to haul coal. The mine closed in 1971 when a highway was rerouted over its entrance. The film shows what working in the coal mine was like by following the activities of four miners, all more than 60 years old, who had spent most of their lives underground. The New Gladstone was operated seasonally, during the fall and winter months, to supply local heating needs. The daily output of the mine, with only four men working, was about 16 tons. During the spring and summer, the miners had other jobs such as farming.

The mine's low roof, typical of Iowa coal mines, was five feet high, so miners had to work in cramped positions all day long. Because of low clearances, the New Gladstone Mine didn't use just any ponies—it used Shetland ponies, which are shorter than other breeds and thus better able to fit through the passages. Although ponies were used, the mining techniques employed at the New Gladstone weren't otherwise all that primitive. For example, an electric cutting machine was used to undercut the coal seam in this longwall mine—not hand picks. Nor was the last pony mine the last coal mine in Iowa. The last underground coal mine in Iowa, highly mechanized, closed in 1981.

In the grainy film, the mine's coal seam glistens like polished steel. The miners wear carbide lamps on cloth caps, a form of illumination and headgear that is now illegal in mines. Their lunch pails unappetizingly resemble paint cans. The patient photographer somehow captured the exact moment when the undercut coal wedge fell, to be broken up and stacked into wooden coal cars. Ponies didn't haul coal out of the mine; they merely hauled it to the base of the slope, where a motorized winch took over. At the surface, the coal was dumped into trucks for local distribution.

After watching the film, you can enter the Last Pony Mine itself. Actually, it's the former water reservoir for the steam boiler that used to heat the post office, cleverly made over to resemble a coal mine! A hole was knocked through the thick brick wall, creating a rugged-looking entrance. A mining mural was painted around this opening. You must stoop to enter, but the interior is of standing height. The mine contains a carved wooden pony pulling a wooden coal car.

The second, adjacent room re-creates an earlier phase of mining history, back when hand picks were used. Appropriately, the room housing this display is the former coal storage room of the post office, complete with a scuttle, or opening in the wall, for coal deliveries. The space under a long table represents the mine passage itself, with the underside of the table representing the roof of the mine passage, which you are not meant to enter. A miner mannequin lies on its side, undercutting the seam with a hand pick. Coal chunks up to two feet across litter the floor.

The museum contains other mine-related displays. One entire wall of the basement is devoted to mining maps and historic photos, many of which depict scenes from the New Gladstone Mine. If you are nostalgic about the Last Pony Mine, a 1967 newspaper clipping invites you to be equally sentimental about the "Last of the Shale Dumps." Shale waste rock from local mines was baked by fires in these dumps, turning it a distinctive red color. Afterward, the shale was used as a surfacing material on county roads.

A large wall map of Appanoose County coal mine locations indicates that most of the mines were (not surprisingly) concentrated along railways and around Centerville itself and that some individual mines underlie more than one square mile of land surface. A nearby chart lists the names of 357 mines that were thought to operate in the county at one time or another. The number of listed mines is a bit misleading because sometimes an old mine, or part of it, resumed operations under a new name. Despite the questionable number, it's estimated that there were more than twice as many coal mines in Appanoose County than in any other county in the state, although the total coal output of a few other counties was greater.

Finally, you can examine a tabletop model of the town of Mystic, complete with little wooden buildings. Mystic is the coal-mining town northwest of Centerville that gave its name to the county's predominant coal seam. A four-foot-high model of a coal tipple from the Diamond Mine, once situated near the town of Numa southwest of Centerville, sits nearby.

Directions: Located in the former red brick post office on State Highway 2 in downtown Centerville.

Season/hours: Sunday, 1:30 to 4:00 p.m., Memorial Day through October, or by appointment. Fee.

Precautions: None.

Amenities: Downtown Centerville.

Contact: Historical and Coal Mining Museum, 100 West Maple Street (State Highway 2), Centerville, IA 52544. Phone: (641) 856-8040.

35
Boone County Historical Center
Boone County

I N THE 1830S, Nathan Boone, son of Daniel Boone, led a regiment of dragoons (mounted infantry) to explore the Des Moines River valley. The path is now a marked series of roads called the **Dragoon Trail.** By 1835, he ended up in what is now Boone County, which is named after him. The Boone County Historical Center, housed in an old Masonic temple in Boone, the county seat, contains a display commemorating this historic exploration. The museum also features a coal mine replica, which recalls the county's bountiful coal deposits.

Coal was mined in Boone County for use by blacksmiths as early as the 1840s, but the industry really took off with the arrival of the Chicago & North Western Railroad in 1866. The town of Boone became the Iowa headquarters for that railroad, which had many "captive" coal mines, operated by and for the benefit of the railroads.

Basically, there were two coal seams in Boone County, the upper vein, which was more productive and which this coal mine replica seeks to illustrate, and a lower vein, reached by deep shafts. The exhibit replicates an early Boone County slope coal mine. The timbering of the mine replica was installed by a former miner. A wooden coal car is depicted emerging from the mine, but it blocks the entrance, so the mine is not meant to be entered.

Next to the replica mine is a display of mining tools and photos of mines that once operated below the city of Boone itself. On the wall are maps of local railroad towns. A display devoted to Kate Shelley explains how she saved the Chicago & North Western's Midnight Express from a watery grave on a stormy night in 1881 by crawling across a high trestle to warn the train that another bridge in the vicinity had washed out. (You can experience firsthand the dizzying heights of these trestles by riding the **Boone and Scenic Valley Railroad**; call (800) 626-0319.)

Wildlife mounts in the Natural History Room show how dramatically the environment of Iowa has changed since the influx of white settlers in the nineteenth century. Another display contains mounted fish from the Des Moines River. Read about Carl Fritz-Henning, an early "tree hugger" who kept getting embroiled in controversy as he campaigned for land and wildlife conservation. He was the chief promoter of nearby **Ledges State Park**, established in 1924. (It has often been said that Ledges State Park "looks" like it should contain caves, but none have been found there to date!)

One display addresses the much earlier occupants of Boone County. The Boone Mound excavation of 1908 found artifacts from the long-vanished Hopewell culture. Hopewell mounds are rarely found this far west in Iowa. A mammoth tusk found in a local streambed is also displayed.

There are two nearby attractions that should interest people who want to learn more about the area's underground features. **The Voas Geology Museum**, (515) 465-3577, located near Minburn in adjacent Dallas County, contains an extensive rock, mineral, and fossil collection put together by the Voas family. A display features the local coal-mining industry, including mining tools. There are artifacts from Angus, the best-known coal-mining ghost town in Boone County, which thrived in the 1880s. The fossil collection contains "coal palm trees." (Coal trees were not true palm trees—those appeared much later in geologic history.) A sectioned and polished trunk of the botanically more advanced Cordaites coal tree is also on display.

Specimens of products from other kinds of Iowa mines are on display, along with Keokuk geodes. Artifacts from the Redfield archaeological dig document the prehistoric occupants of Dallas County. The

A replica of a hill-slope mine, of the type that provided coal for the Chicago & North Western Railroad, is featured at the Boone County Historical Museum.

Voas Museum is being remodeled and plans to add a coal forest diorama, an artificial glacier, and a blacklight booth containing fluorescent minerals. The Voas site includes farmland that features restored prairie potholes and other habitats.

Springbrook State Park is located in neighboring Guthrie County, southwest of Boone County. Coal seams exposed in the bluffs of the Middle Raccoon River gave rise to many small coal mines within what is now the park. Coal was mined here seasonally for local heating needs from 1894 to 1941. No open shafts remain, however. Guthrie County is notable as the location of Iowa's sole dinosaur discovery.

Directions: Just off U.S. Highway 30; follow the signs.

Season/hours: Monday through Saturday, 1:00 to 5:00 p.m., June through August; Monday to Friday in April, May, and September to November. Fee.

Precautions: None.

Amenities: Downtown Boone.

Contact: Boone County Historical Center, 602 Story Street, Boone, IA 50036. Phone: (515) 432-1907. Web site: http://homepages.isunet.net/bchs/ BCHSHistoricalCenter.htm

36

Madrid Historical Museum
Boone County

D ESPITE ITS SPANISH-sounding name, the town of Madrid claims to be the oldest continuously inhabited Swedish set-tlement west of the Mississippi River. The community bestrides a string of coal mines that once operated along the Des Moines River in southern Boone County. The largest of them, Scandia No. 4, was located just south of town. The Scandia Coal Company had five other mines in the area, which was also the site of such notable mines as High Bridge, Moran, Phildia, and Zookspur. So, it's no wonder that the Madrid Historical Museum is home to a simulated coal mine, named, appropriately enough, "Scandia No. 7."

Scandia No. 7 was not the town's first coal mine replica, however. A local mining enthusiast named Leonard Ackerlund built a replica from black tar paper in the basement of a grocery store for the Madrid centennial celebration of 1983. It remained on display until the building was razed years later.

In 1992, a basement was excavated under the old library to create space for the present mining replica and exhibits. You enter the base-ment mine through a black plywood tunnel 50 feet long, with rough-hewn timbering fashioned by a former mine timberman. The rubble masonry walls of the basement are painted black, and viewed from a distance they do indeed resemble a coal seam! The tunnel contains tracks and wooden coal cars heaped with coal. The far end of the tunnel is made to resemble a mine face. Instead of the usual man-nequin, miner's clothes have been draped over a sort of metal skeleton made from coal augers. The sign says it all—"Iowa Coal Miners Were Iron Men!" Advertisements from the *Coal Field Directory* frame this unusual exhibit.

The outer side of the plywood mine tunnel is plastered with yel-lowed newspaper clippings, including an unusual article about the "Bjuv stegocefal," a fossil that superficially resembles an alligator, found in the Bjuv coal mines of Sweden. There are also photos of Madrid's sister city, Madrid, New Mexico—another former mining town with its own mining museum!

Also on display are fossil plants, labeled "coal palm trees," in recog-

Gypsum Mining and the Cardiff Giant

The pioneering geologist David Dale Owen, traveling up the Des Moines River in 1849, vividly described the Fort Dodge gypsum deposits for the first time. He wrote that it was the most important bed of plaster-stone known west of the Appalachian Chain . . .

> . . . *It is seen at intervals for three miles, exposed on both sides of the Des Moines, in mural faces of from eighteen to twenty-five feet, always overlying pink shales, from beneath which copious springs of excellent water issue. It has been traced in the ravines, back from the river . . . where it is finally lost under the deep alluvion of the vast plains that stretch away to the west.*

Not surprisingly, Fort Dodge was subsequently dubbed "Gypsum City."

Initially, the local Jurassic-age gypsum was quarried in the valleys, where it outcropped. Beginning in 1895, gypsum mining shifted underground. In the early twentieth century, with advances in mechanized equipment, surface mining returned. Fort Dodge isn't the only place where gypsum is mined in Iowa. Near the town of Sperry in southeastern Iowa, you can see the headframe of Iowa's deepest mine, at more than six hundred feet.

Fort Dodge gypsum was first used for building stone. The first plaster mill opened in 1872, supplying gypsum for stucco. The most important use of gypsum today is for the manufacture of wallboard, or sheetrock.

The local gypsum also figured prominently in one of the most notorious hoaxes in our nation's history. In 1868, George Hull arranged for a huge block of gypsum to be sculpted into the shape of a naked man in agony. The stone giant, 10.5 feet long, was given simulated skin pores with a needle-tipped hammer and artificially aged with sulfuric acid. It even appeared to have blue veins, but in fact, such discolorations are characteristic of the parent gypsum deposit.

Hull secretly buried the giant on a farm near Cardiff, New York, where it was "discovered" a year later during the digging of a well. A tent was erected, and the farm owner, who was in on the scheme, began charging admission. The poet Ralph Waldo Emerson pronounced the appearance of the giant as "beyond our depth." The great showman P. T. Barnum offered a huge sum for it. When he was refused, Barnum had his own giant carved—and declared that the original was a fake! Historian James Taylor Dunn later dubbed the Cardiff Giant "this American belly-laugh in stone."

The original Cardiff Giant is on display at the Farmer's Museum in Cooperstown, New York, but the **Fort Dodge Museum,** (515) 573-4231, has a replica. For a unique way to experience other aspects of gypsum mining, visit the **Mineral City Mill and Grill,** 2621 5th Avenue South (U.S. Highway 20 Business), which has many historical mining photos on the walls. The booths are framed by square-set timbering, similar to that used in real mines. Get up close to natural gypsum outcrops in **Snell Park,** or have a glimpse of the extensive mined-out gypsum "badlands" on the south side of Fort Dodge, by following 22nd Street (becomes Vincent Drive) south along the banks of Gypsum Creek.

nition that pieces of fossil coal trees are occasionally found by local residents in the streambeds around Madrid.

A tabletop model of the Zerr & Burke Mine, crafted by Martin Burke, a former coal miner, is on display. Burlap cloth is used to represent the hillside on which it sits. A coal tipple bears the name of the Sugar Valley Coal Company. The cutaway view of the mine is wonderful for understanding how a longwall mine operated.

The **Clay Castle Museum,** a collection of more than one thousand dolls, occupies the first floor of the museum building. Many of them are porcelain dolls—hence the name "clay." The mining theme is continued here too, with displays of mining-related scrapbooks and cabinets of rocks, minerals, and fossils.

Directions: Take Exit 102 on Interstate 35, north of Des Moines, and head west on State Highway 210.

Season/hours: By appointment only. Free, donations appreciated.

Length: 50 feet.

Precautions: None.

Amenities: Downtown Madrid.

Contact: Madrid Historical Museum, 109 West Second, Madrid, IA 50156. Phone: (515) 795-3249.

37

Jasper County Historical Museum
Jasper County

T HE TOWN OF Newton bills itself as the "Washing Machine Capital of the World," and the Jasper County Historical Museum certainly reflects that heritage, containing several rooms chock-full of washing machines built by the Maytag Company since 1907 and its predecessors, including the One Minute Manufacturing Company. The contraptions range from crude, wooden barrel washers to the latest models, complete with microchips. But I couldn't help wondering whether the emphasis on cleaning clothes came from an even earlier local industry, one that dirtied clothes more thoroughly than just about any other—coal mining!

In a far corner of the museum, beyond rows of gleaming white washers, you will find a coal mine replica containing a male mannequin covered with soot. (All the other coal mine replicas that I have seen in Iowa contain female mannequins—apparently because they are much more readily obtained from store-front displays!) The grimy miner, wearing a cloth cap with a carbide light, is kneeling in a four-foot-high coal seam and using a frame drill to create a hole that will be packed with explosives. Behind him is a coal car on rails. Spread out on the floor are his lunch pail, pick, augers, tampers, and other tools. These items came from the Sam Bolens & Sons Mine, which operated locally from 1919 to 1940.

To the right of the mine replica is a model of a Warren Grove Coal Mine tipple, which shows how mine cars were winched to the top of the structure and dropped their load of coal into waiting trucks below. This particular coal mine, located north of the town of Monroe, was the last underground mine in Jasper County. On the wall to the left of the replica, there is a map of the locations of the county's coal mines.

A wall chart of Jasper County railroads—a web of toy tracks glued onto cardboard—indicates how important railroads were to the coal mining industry in the county. Most of the mines were "captive" mines operated by and for the railroads. The display includes railroad items, the most unique of which is a collection of railroad nails—

In a corner of the Jasper County Historical Museum, most of which is devoted to Maytag washing machines, a miner wears dirty clothes that could provide the ultimate cleaning test!

numbered nails pounded into railroad ties of different kinds of wood to track how well they held up under constant use.

Other local industries, such as the Newton Foundry, are featured in this corner of the museum. Brick and tile plants once abounded in Jasper County, and a display contains samples of locally made bricks and drain tiles. The museum also contains Victorian-period rooms and, on the lower level, a Native American diorama, with displays of agricultural tools. A 40-foot bas-relief near the entrance to the museum nicely sums up the history of Jasper County.

Newton is also the home of the Maytag Dairy Farm. During World War II, when the nation was cut off from French imports, a domestic blue cheese industry sprang up here to replace the unavailable Roquefort. A ripening cave, 68 feet long and 15 feet wide, was dug in a hillside.

Although the coal mine replica itself is located in Newton, the most important mining town in Jasper County was actually **Colfax** (Exit 155 on Interstate 80, just west of Newton). The first commercial mine opened here in 1871, supplying coal to the Rock Island Railroad. Colfax was most famous, however, as Iowa's "Spring City." In 1875, while drilling for coal, workmen tapped into artesian water. The high mineral content of the water suggested great medicinal value. More wells were drilled, and Colfax gained a reputation as a spa, eventually being dubbed "the Carlsbad of America" and "the Saratoga of the

West." Several grand hotels sprang up to capitalize on the mineral water trade, the most famous of which was the Hotel Colfax. A splendid example of the California Mission Revival architectural style in Iowa, this former hotel features a creamy stucco exterior and a red tile roof. At one time it was called the "Pig Palace" because pigs were housed there, and it later became one of the largest alcoholic rehabilitation centers in the United States. It is now the Salvatorian Novitiate (private). Most of the so-called springs in Colfax were actually drilled wells. You can sample the waters at the pavilion in **Mineral Springs Park** (Front and Walnut).

A related attraction is the **Old Jumbo Well**, commemorated by a bronze plaque on a granite boulder on the corner of 8th Avenue and 8th Street in the town of Belle Plaine. While drilling a fire department well in 1886, an artesian gusher broke forth so powerful that it took more than a year to bring under control. The well was acclaimed the 8th wonder of the world and was reported in European newspapers of the day.

Directions: From Exit 164 on Interstate 80, just east of Des Moines, go north one half mile on U.S. Highway 6 to the first stoplight, turn right and double back along the service road.

Season/hours: Daily, 1:00 to 4:30 p.m., May 1 to October 1; otherwise by appointment. Fee.

Length: 50 feet.

Precautions: None.

Amenities: Research library.

Contact: Jasper County Historical Museum, 1700 South 15th Avenue West, Newton, IA 50208. Phone: (641) 792-9118.

Brick School Museum
Keokuk County

I N 1857, a couple of miners traveling across the prairies of south-eastern Iowa came to a crude sign affixed to a wooden post that read, "To the Coal Banks." They soon after arrived at a modest dwelling, the start of what would become the town of What Cheer. The area contained rich seams of coal, so it's not too surprising that the town adopted a name associated with coal mining. ("What Cheer," pronounced "watcher" by locals, was a miner's salutation that basically means "How do you do?") However, it wasn't until the arrival of the railroad in 1879 that the area's coal industry boomed. More than a hundred mines eventually opened; a good example is the Northwestern Fuel Company, which supplied coal for the Chicago & North Western Railroad—known as the "Pumpkin Vine" because of its winding route. In 1888, a second, deeper vein of coal was

A mannequin at the window beckons visitors into the Brick School Museum in What Cheer.

discovered during the sinking of a well.

The town of What Cheer is built on several hills, around which Coal Creek winds its way. There were eight mining suburbs, called "camps," in the vicinity. Old accounts tell how, when viewed from the hilltops in the evening, the miners looked like fireflies returning from the mines with their pit lamps. In 1887, What Cheer witnessed what may have been one of the first significant labor disputes in Iowa. Mine owners attempted to break a bitter strike by bringing in African-American miners, but after a strong protest by the strikers, they were escorted back out of town.

Most of the mines closed by 1900 when all the easily mined coal had been exhausted. Associated industries also came to an end. The What Cheer Tool Company, for example, supposedly the largest manufacturer of mining tools in the world, closed in 1926. There were 50 other businesses in What Cheer, enough for the town to be dubbed "Little Chicago."

When coal mining ended, What Cheer turned to its clay deposits for a livelihood. The scenic lake in **Griffin Park**, south of town, was created from a former clay pit. The What Cheer Clay Products Company became the largest manufacturer of sewer pipe in the Midwest, also manufacturing vast amounts of drain tile for farm fields. Much of downtown What Cheer, including the Brick School Museum, which has a coal-mining exhibit, is made from clay from these deposits.

On the first floor of the Brick School Museum, a glass case contains Jobe Grudgings's mining tools. Grudgings was a local miner who continued to dig the hills for heating coal long after others had given up such work. The Grudgings mine, the last one in What Cheer, closed in 1942.

The main coal-mining exhibit is found on the second floor. Visitors are enthusiastically beckoned into the room by a waving miner mannequin. You can almost hear him utter the old miner's salutation, "What Cheer." Several rows of tables display a wide variety of mining tools, from hand picks to augers. Augers were used to drill holes in the coal face, and the holes were then packed with explosives. Personal gear of the miners, such as lamps and lunch pails, is tucked in among big chunks of coal, dynamite boxes, and gas masks. The rest of the room is filled with agricultural implements. This museum does not contain electric coal cutters and more advanced mining equipment like you would find in other museums because major coal mining ended in What Cheer by the time these innovations became widespread.

Today, the town is perhaps best known for the What Cheer Opera House (on the National Register of Historic Places) and its annual flea market, the largest in Iowa, held at the Keokuk County Fairgrounds.

Directions: From State Highway 21 (Barnes), which runs
north to south through town, look for the big, red
former school building on the hill east of the
road. Turn east onto Broadway, then south on
Burlington.

Season/hours: Open July 4th and by appointment. Fee.

Precautions: None.

Amenities: Downtown What Cheer.

Contact: What Cheer Brick School Museum, Box 94, What
Cheer, IA 50268. Phone: (641) 634-2605.

John L. Lewis Mining and Labor Museum
Lucas County

THIS MUSEUM opened in 1990 to commemorate John L.
Lewis (1880–1969), longtime president of the United Mines
Workers of America (UMWA) and advocate of miners' rights.
Lewis was born of Welsh immigrants in the coal-mining camp at
Cleveland, a mile east of Lucas. Although he lived most of his life in
Washington, D.C., he learned firsthand about mining right here in
Iowa.

You should first enter the 40-seat theater and watch the half-hour
video about the life of Lewis, narrated by a youthful Mike Wallace.
Other videos available for viewing include The King of Coal, which
gives a general overview of Iowa coal mining, and The Last Pony
Mine, a classic documentary about the last mine in the United States
to use ponies to haul coal. The library has an impressive collection of
newspaper clippings about the life of Lewis.

About half the museum is devoted exclusively to Lewis's life. Begin
your tour in the room devoted to "Old Lucas," which contains memorabilia of the hometown of Lewis, founded by the Burlington &
Missouri River Railroad in 1867. Nearby, a deluxe HO-scale model of
Lucas as it appeared in about 1900 occupies a glass-top case. It shows
the tipple of the Big Hill Coal Company (1879–1907), one of two coal
mines in the town itself where Lewis and his father once worked.

The John L. Lewis Museum in Lucas has a splendid collection of Iowa coal mining artifacts and exhibits about the life of the great labor leader.

Company housing, a cluster of white miner's cabins known as White Chapel, is also shown. A map behind the display shows the town of Lucas with area mines.

The story of Lewis's battle on behalf of coal miners begins at the life-size bronze statue of the great labor leader, commissioned especially for the museum by the UMWA. He stands in a typically defiant oratorical pose, like a great tree of the Coal Age. A cartoon gallery, aisles of clippings about labor history, and reproductions of photos from the National Archives in Washington, D.C., tell the story.

The UMWA was formed in 1890 to combat the many unfair labor practices that mine owners and operators regularly engaged in. Grievances among miners were many. Imagine working 50 years of your life in a coal seam two and a half feet high! The first campaign was for an eight-hour workday. It was common for miners to go underground before sunrise and exit the mine after sunset, so they would not see daylight all week. Others pushed to get union check-weighmen to make sure that the company weigh boss, who weighed the coal cars as they came out of the mine, didn't shortchange them. This was especially important since a miner was paid for tonnage of coal mined, not hours worked per se. Nor were miners paid for dead work—activities essential to the operation of the mine, but not directly involved with the actual mining of the coal. Digging the floor down, for example, so that track could be laid, was essentially unproductive work. The circumstances of the pay itself were also an issue.

"Long pay"—being paid only once a month—or being paid in scrip redeemable only at the company store, were additional causes of discontent.

But despite several years of effort by the UMWA, many of the old abuses crept back into the industry. Mine operators often ignored contracts they had signed and went unpunished because of ineffectual labor laws.

In 1933, labor unions suddenly achieved a totally new and robust legal status under Roosevelt's New Deal. Lewis, who as president of the UMWA since 1920 had been accused of vote rigging and slothful inactivity, now saw the chance of a lifetime. He initiated union recruiting drives that swept through the nation's coalfields. Union ranks swelled to unprecedented numbers. Even captive coal mines, wholly owned by entities such as railroads and steel companies, were successfully unionized. The UMWA established a welfare and retirement fund, built miners' hospitals, and provided health care for its members.

Lewis was only beginning his march to even greater power. He championed the notion of industrial unionism, the idea that every worker in a particular industry, no matter what his or her job, should belong to the same union. This was a radical departure from the craft unionism practiced by the American Federation of Labor (AFL). Lewis succeeded in transforming the UMWA into an industrial union, whereupon the practice soon spread to the automotive and steel industries. Lewis formed the Committee for Industrial Organization (CIO) within the AFL in 1935 and became president of the CIO three years later.

Lewis overreached himself, however, when he broke with Roosevelt by endorsing his Republican rival in the 1940 presidential election. When Roosevelt won, Lewis interpreted the victory as a repudiation of his own leadership and resigned from the CIO. And when Lewis called a strike in 1943 during the height of World War II, it was seen as a strike against the government rather than against mine operators, and some people regarded him as a traitor. Yet Lewis's power within the labor movement continued to grow.

However, by 1948, especially with the invention of a complete mining device, called the Joy machine (after the Joy Manufacturing Company of Pittsburgh), with its rotating drums to eat into the coal seam and its claw-like arms to scoop the fragments, the coal industry was becoming increasingly mechanized, resulting in a steady decline in employment, and hence the power of the UMWA. Unexpectedly, Lewis supported the increasing mechanization of mining, arguing that it reduced the backbreaking labor involved.

The UMWA resorted to questionable practices during the 1950s to boost membership. Electric utilities, burning coal to produce steam,

Iowa Gold Fever

There were many gold rushes in nineteenth-century America, and Iowa had its own share, albeit on a more modest scale. Many streams in Iowa, when panned, have yielded small amounts of genuine gold, but there are no gold-bearing rocks or mother lodes in the state. The gold that has been found derives from glacial drift, having been carried down from the north by glaciers. Streams crossing the drift concentrated the heavy gold particles into placer deposits.

The first report of gold in Iowa came in 1853, after many miners had already departed for California, where gold had been discovered a few years earlier. An innkeeper in Eldora announced the discovery of gold on his farm along the Iowa River. The fanfare attracted 3,000 miners, but they all left disappointed, some later sending him death threats. Many believe it was just a scheme to keep his inn busy!

In 1877, gold was found in the black sands of the Iowa River near Steamboat Rock, just upstream from Eldora. Also, gold was supposedly found in Bear Creek, causing the Ottumwa Gold Rush, which led to the formation of the Wapello Gold Mining Company in 1881. But after due analysis, it was found not to be gold. Pioneers found gold along Moine Creek, which flows through Brush Creek Canyon State Preserve (see Section I). In the 1920s, the town of Graettinger was called "The Gold Mine City of Iowa," but nothing definite panned out in that case either. The appropriately named town of Klondike on the Big Sioux River was the location of Iowa's only viable gold mine—again based on river deposits.

More fantastic, however, is the story of the "lost gold cave" on the Volga River in northeastern Iowa. One day, the story goes, a Winnebago chief blindfolded a miner and lowered him into a cave on a rope. When the blindfold was removed the miner was amazed to see that the walls were made of gold and that there were 12 pots of gold dust on the floor. After being returned home, he searched in vain for the gold cave.

The level-headed advice given by many newspaper editors at the time of these gold rushes was that the real gold of Iowa was to be found in its agricultural wealth, and they advised would-be miners to stay home and farm the land. Indeed, many of the little gold rushes were likely nothing more than fraudulent schemes to boost land values.

were becoming the principal users of coal, and the Tennessee Valley Authority (TVA), run by the federal government, became the largest coal purchaser in the world. The UMWA put pressure on small, nonunion mines in TVA country to join, often using violence to intimidate mine owners and workers alike. The small mines could not bid competitively for the TVA coal contracts because they could not afford to pay the higher wages that resulted from unionization. The

UMWA was repeatedly sued under the Sherman Antitrust Act for having conspired with the larger coal producers to drive these small, nonunionized mines out of business. In 1960, Lewis retired as president of the UMWA, a position he had held for 40 years.

The other half of the museum is devoted to Iowa coal mining in general. One exhibit shows the evolutionary sequence from peat to lignite, bituminous, and anthracite coals. Also displayed are a petrified log that was found 80 feet down in a coal mine and a 1962 clipping about "Fossil Farm" near Knoxville, where the fossils of many coal trees have been found. A dinosaur footprint from Utah, filled with coal deposit, and "pyrite suns"—radiating crystals of pyrite, a mineral often found in coal—are displayed. The Coal Figurine Collection shows an assortment of figurines cunningly sculpted from coal.

A glass case contains perhaps the finest collection of miner's lamps in Iowa. The display proceeds chronologically, beginning with candles and proceeding to the "Miner's Needle or Sticking Tommy" and sunshine lamps. With a "Lard Oil Pit Lamp and Pail," the pail was used to melt the oil, which looks like yellow beeswax, to pour into the lamps. It was good to see an exhibit of the modern brass Auto Lite carbide headlamp, widely used by cavers today. A diagram shows how the lamp works. Water drips down from an upper reservoir onto the carbide, generating acetylene gas. The strength of the flame is controlled by adjusting the drip rate of the water.

Another exhibit features safety lamps, self-rescuer cartridges, gas testers, and carbide canisters. Safety lamps were designed to prevent explosions by having the flame burn behind a screen. The heat of the flame was dissipated by the glowing screen, so it could not pass outward to ignite an explosion. Also on display is a "Union Jack," a caltrop that was placed on roads during strikes to puncture the tires of scabs. Caltrops are devices consisting of four metal points, one of which is always projecting upward to inflict damage. Many miners had British roots, and they named these wicked little items "Union Jacks" because their pattern resembled that of the British flag.

The museum's ample tool collection contains coal wedges, pony shoes, molefoot drillbits, black powder chargers, a breast drill with a six-foot auger, fuse needles, hand picks, and miner's lunch pails. The lunch pail had three compartments, the upper two for food and the lower one to hold water for drinking and washing and for the ever-thirsty carbide lamps. There is a Cripple Creek gold-ore car from Colorado, along with a wooden half-ton coal car. A mannequin representing a child stands in a corner, with a poignant reminder that the legal age limit to work in the mines rose from 10 years in 1874 to 12 years in 1880 and 14 years in 1906.

The museum has a gift shop where you can purchase coal figurines and other souvenirs. Outside the museum there is a dirt car, hoist, fan, and an electric Sullivan coal cutter, all of which were used in the New Gladstone Mine near Centerville. Finally, visit the marker commemorating John L. Lewis in Lucas City Park.

Directions: Two blocks north of U.S. Highway 34, in Lucas.

Season/hours: Monday through Saturday, 9:00 a.m. to 3:00 p.m., April 15 through October 15. Allow one to three hours to see the exhibits. Fee.

Precautions: None.

Amenities: Gift shop.

Contact: John L. Lewis Mining and Labor Museum, P.O. Box 3, 102 Division Street, Lucas, IA 50151. Phone: (641) 766-6831.

Lucas County Historical Museum
Lucas County

IN THE JOHN L. LEWIS Building in Chariton (behind the A. J. Stephens House, which is on the National Register of Historic Places), you'll find the Lucas County Historical Museum. On the first floor, amid the eclectic collection of nineteenth-century items, is a glass case containing local mining photos. The mines in this county drew their coal from the widespread Whitebreast seam. The last coal mine in the county, the Nebraska-Iowa Mine, closed in 1923.

The basement contains a coal mine replica flanked by a mannequin dressed as a miner. A painting over the entrance depicts events from the history of coal mining in Lucas County, with John L. Lewis himself presiding over the scene. You pass through a short plywood tunnel painted black and arrive at a corner of the basement, where the brickwork is also painted black to represent the working face of a coal mine. The mine, littered with coal, contains a drill assembly, a wooden coal car, and a canary cage hanging from the roof.

Outside the mine, a display entitled "A Set of Mining Tools" emphasizes how each miner was regarded as an independent contractor who had to furnish his own tools. A model of a coal tipple stands nearby.

A portrait of John L. Lewis looms above the coal mine replica in the Lucas County Historical Museum.

Apart from that, the lower level includes, as described in a brochure, "a country store, butcher shop, doctor's office, broom factory, rug loom, a machinery display and miniature barn, doll house, circus, and log cabins."

Directions:	Take U.S. Highway 34 Business through Chariton. Turn north on 17th Street, go one block.
Season/hours:	Tuesday through Friday, 1:00 to 4:00 p.m., Memorial Day to October 1. Free.
Length:	30 feet.
Precautions:	None.
Amenities:	The Cinder Path, the first Rails-to-Trails path in Iowa, on an old right-of-way, begins in Chariton.
Contact:	Lucas County Historical Museum, 123 North 17th Street, Chariton, IA 50049. Phone: (641) 774-4464.

41

Melcher-Dallas Coal Mining and Heritage Museum
Marion County

BETWEEN THE mid-nineteenth century and the end of World War II, coal was king in Marion County. It all began in Coalport, which became the county's first coal-mining town even before the advent of railroads. Because of the coal outcrops along the banks of the Des Moines River, the community developed as an important fueling stop for steamboats plying its waters. Coalport was later inundated by the rising waters of the Red Rock Reservoir ("Iowa's Largest Lake") and a prominent white church is all that remains of the town today.

Over the years, more than five hundred underground and surface mines operated in Marion County, some of them so close together that they "blew into each other." Two coal seams were commonly mined here. The upper seam, about 3.5 feet thick, was exposed along the banks of White Breast Creek, a tributary of the Des Moines River. The thickness of the deeper seam ranged from four to seven feet. The two seams were exploited by slope and shaft mines, respectively; the deepest of the mines was two hundred feet below the surface.

Most of the county's mines were exhausted by the end of World War II, leaving nothing but a pile of shale for a tombstone. Sometimes even the shale was hauled away to pave roads. Another mine came to an untimely end for quite a different reason: water burst through the roof one night, filling the entire mine.

Through it all, the neighboring towns of Melcher and Dallas played a vital part in Marion County's coal industry. Melcher was incorporated in 1913 after the Rock Island Railroad extended its tracks to get coal for its locomotives. In addition to the railroads, another big coal purchaser was the Central Iowa Fuel Company. Dallas, immediately to the north, had been founded much earlier, in 1845. The towns merged in 1986 and are often referred to as the Twin Cities, or "MD" for short.

The miners here often led a desperate existence. Many of them lived in squalid, dirt-floored shacks in a place called "Shack Town" just outside Melcher. In the summer, when there was little demand for heating coal, some miners commuted 50 miles to Newton to build washing machines at the Maytag factory. Out-of-work miners fished and gardened in the summer and hunted rabbits in the winter. Sometimes a group of miners who had been laid off got together and dug their own mine. Not surprisingly, the area was a fertile recruiting ground for the United Mine Workers of America.

The Melcher-Dallas Coal Mining and Heritage Museum, located in the historic, red-brick Old Miner's Hall, pays tribute to the local miners. One whole wall is occupied by a huge mural of a coal tipple. (The tiny painted mules, however, give an inflated impression of the size of the tipple.) There are displays of miners' hats, carbide lamps, mole teeth (drill bits), mule shoes, and so forth. Another display features Tom Wignall, the owner and operator of Lovilia Coal Company (which was actually located in Monroe County, adjacent to the south). Wignall was widely recognized for bringing about improvements in mechanized coal mining. The company's Lovilia No. 3 became Iowa's first "mechanical mine." It was also the first roof-bolted mine in Iowa, eliminating the need for timbering.

After walking down a short flight of steps to an intermediate level, you encounter a reconstructed blacksmith shop. Blacksmiths were important to mines because they shod the mules and repaired coal

A wooden coal car sits in a mine replica at the Melcher-Dallas Coal Mining and Heritage Museum in the town's Old Miner's Hall.

Iowa's Iron Mine

Before 1875, no one really thought that the boulders of iron ore that crowned Iron Hill, near Waukon, in Allamakee County, represented a marketable deposit. In that year, an analysis of the ore showed that it was hematite, an oxide of iron. In 1882, serious exploratory work began. Dozens of shafts were sunk to determine the thickness of the ore body. No ledge of iron ore was found, but it was estimated that there was enough ore in boulder form to last a century. The main problem was getting it to market. If the ore could be transported to the Mississippi River, it could be floated in barges to Dubuque for smelting.

The Waukon Iron Company, founded in 1900, mined the ore from an open pit. Unfortunately, tailings from the operation filled local streambeds, causing floods. Farmers began legal proceedings and the mine closed in 1902. The Iowa Hematite Railway Company was founded that same year to transport the ore but it vanished without laying an inch of track.

A few years later the Missouri Iron Company took over the mine. A railroad spur was built from the mine to nearby Waukon, where it joined the Milwaukee Road. The tracks ran down the scenic Paint Creek valley to Waukon Junction, where the ore was processed. There were many sharp curves along the way and the place was infested with rattlesnakes—"covering the ground like a plate of spaghetti" according to one engineer!

Having at last solved all its problems, the mine was poised to take off. Unfortunately, World War I intervened. The United States Railroad Administration took over the allocation of rail cars and because the mine was deemed secondary to those of the Mesabi Range in Minnesota, no cars were allowed to ship the ore. The mine languished.

cars. In the same room is a collection of miners' picks and pails. Continue down the wooden steps into the mine replica. Wooden lagging covers the walls of the 40-foot-long tunnel, which contains a wooden coal car on rails. The tunnel leads to the "working face" of the mine, where a drill is set up. Another realistic touch is that the dampness of the basement even recaptures some of the odors of a coal mine!

Like other coal mine replicas around the state, this one features a toy canary in a cage. In the days before electronic gas meters, canaries were used to detect the presence of carbon monoxide, also called "white damp," in mines. Owing to their high metabolic rate, canaries were quickly overcome by even small concentrations of the gas, alerting miners and allowing them to escape.

The museum also has a small theater where you can watch a 14-minute video, When King Coal Reigned in Iowa, and a 90-minute video interview in which retired local coal miners swap stories and "chew the fat" around a potbellied stove. Learn why a miner taps the ceiling when he enters the mine at the beginning of his shift (to check its integrity) and such arcane details as why mules were preferred to horses in mines (a horse raises its head if its ears touch the ceiling, whereas a mule ducks). The videos can be purchased in the gift shop.

Directions: At the northwest corner of the Melcher town square, in the historic, red brick Old Miner's Hall.

Season/hours: Saturday and Sunday, 1:00 to 4:00 p.m., Memorial Day to Labor Day. Free.

Length: 40 feet.

Precautions: None.

Amenities: Gift shop. The annual "Coal Miner's Day" is held in June.

Contact: Melcher-Dallas Coal Mining and Heritage Museum, North Main, Melcher-Dallas, IA 50163. Phone: (641) 947-5651.

Monroe County Historical Museum
Monroe County

I T'S AMAZING to look at old photos of Buxton, showing the town stretching off to the horizon, and realize that almost nothing of this once-bustling community exists today. It has become the most famous mining ghost town in Iowa. The town is commemorated at the Monroe County Historical Museum, located in Albia, 10 miles to the south. Buxton contributed to Monroe County's position as the state's all-time leading coal-producing county and where the underground mining of coal endured the longest.

The idea for a mine at Buxton began when the Chicago & North Western Railroad, needing a local source of coal for its locomotives, set up the Consolidation Coal Company in the 1870s to mine coal at Muchakinock ("Muchy") in Mahaska County. When a strike broke out, African-Americans were recruited from the South to work the mines. When the output eventually dwindled, J. E. Buxton, the superintendent, decided to extend the railroad tracks southward into

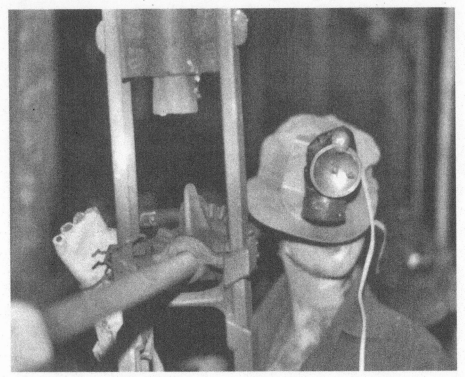

A female manikin operates a drill in one of two coal mine replicas in the Monroe County Historical Museum, Albia.

resource-rich Monroe County. What a good choice it was!

In 1900, the railroad purchased more than 10,000 acres of land, straddling both Mahaska and Monroe Counties. The populace of Muchakinock then moved en masse to the banks of Bluff Creek, where they built the new town that was named for their superintendent. In contrast to the bleakness of many company towns, Buxton was progressive. At its peak, Buxton had 9,000 residents, many of whom were African-American. Reportedly, discrimination was unknown in Buxton, and there were many African-American professional men and women. The nation's first industrial YMCA was established in Buxton, its amenities including pools, tennis courts, concerts, and movies. The town had its own baseball team, the Buxton Wonders, that played around the Midwest.

Consolidation Coal Company's Mine No. 18 became perhaps the largest coal mine in Iowa. Its subterranean engine room alone stretched for two hundred feet. When a strike took place at the mines in 1927, the railroad refused to yield, however, and the town withered away. Many of Buxton's African-American residents relocated to Des Moines. In 1944, what remained of Mine No. 18 was blown up with dynamite.

The Monroe County Historical Museum is housed in Albia's converted interurban-car barn (built in 1910), which in a way is appropriate because electric interurban railways played an important role in the development of the southern Iowa coalfields, allowing the miners to commute. A hallway in the museum has been converted into a simulated mine passage. Two mines, representing different eras, depict the evolution of coal mining in Monroe County. The earlier mine is a cramped, "kneeling," mine furnished with hand picks, shovels, drills, and wooden coal cars. The modern mechanical mine, on the other hand, features coal undercutters, which resemble giant chainsaws, and larger coal cars.

Monroe County's last coal mine closed in 1981 when the Lovilia Coal Company lost its biggest customer, the Iowa Power & Light Company, because of more stringent air-quality laws. The local, high-sulfur coal was uncompetitive with low-sulfur coal from the western United States. A newspaper clipping with the headline, "An era ends in Iowa: The closing of last underground coal mine," tells the sad story. Many other clippings, along with mine maps, adorn the walls.

The former town of **Buxton** itself—without so much as a historical marker—is located 10 miles north of Albia along gravel roads. Take State Highway 5 north to State Highway 137, then to County Road T37, turn west on 340th Street, and go south a short distance on 102nd Lane. About the only remnant of the town is a swaybacked, red-roofed warehouse on the right in the middle of a cornfield. The building is located on private property, so do not trespass! For more information, read the book *Exploring Buried Buxton* by David Gradwohl and Nancy Osborn.

Directions: Located just off State Highway 5 in downtown Albia.

Season/hours: Weekends, 1:00 to 4:00 p.m., May through October, or by appointment. Free.

Length: 30 feet.

Precautions: None.

Amenities: Downtown Albia.

Contact: Monroe County Historical Museum, 114 A-Avenue East, Albia, IA 52531. Phone: (641) 932-7046 or (641) 932-3319.

43

State Historical Society
Polk County

OVER THE YEARS, at least 222 coal mines operated under the city of Des Moines (see sidebar on p.148). Now, the only Des Moines coal mine is found in a museum, and you don't even need a hard hat to tour it. Just drive to the gilded dome of the state capitol and enter the magnificent State Historical Society headquarters, housed in a red granite building across from the capitol.

From the Locust Street entrance, the first exhibit gallery on your left contains "Up from the Depths," an exhibit about the Iowa coal industry that includes a coal mine replica. Displayed in a glass case at the entrance to the mine is a model of the High Bridge tipple. A tipple is a surface structure where mine cars are emptied by being tipped.

In the one-hundred-foot-long imitation coal mine, shiny black plastic simulates the coal seam itself. Between the mine timbers a wooden coal car sits on a narrow-gauge track loaded with real Iowa coal. The "falling wedge" method of longwall mining is explained on a sign. In this technique, the coal seam is undercut and a wedge of coal is allowed to fall down, after which it is broken up and loaded into wooden cars. A display reminds you that the greatest loss of life in Iowa coal mines was from collapsed roofs caused by insufficient timbering—not from dramatic fires or explosions, as is commonly assumed.

Ghostly, white, life-size plaster models of miners toil away in the jet-black coal seam. One miner drills a shot hole, while another mucks, or loads, the coal into a wooden car. The miners are shown in cramped postures because seams were only a few feet high in many Iowa coal mines, and there usually wasn't enough room to stand upright. Try to imagine a whole lifetime of labor spent in that posture, in the light of a flickering lamp!

The opposite wall of this walk-through exhibit is very different. A glass case contains mining tools, including a mole claw (tip of a miner's drill), a black damp lamp for detecting carbon dioxide, various helmet lamps, a pony whip, brace and bits, and a powder ram. At the crank in the wall you are invited to "Take your turn drilling a shot hole into the coal." A photo gallery shows the environmental devastation caused by strip mining, child labor in the mines, and other mine-

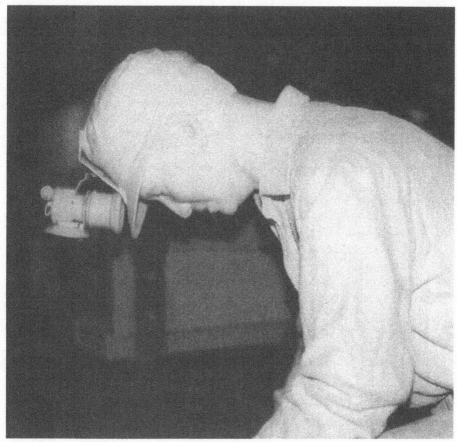

Because of the thinness of Iowa coal seams, miners often spent their whole lives working in a kneeling posture, as suggested by this plaster model at the State Historical Society, Des Moines. Photo by Cindy Doty.

related scenes of social significance.

Upon leaving the mine you are invited to watch an eight-minute video, Up from the Depths, which takes you from the coal forests of the Pennsylvanian Period to the Ottumwa Coal Palace and to Buxton, a once-bustling coal-mining community (see previous entry). The video includes clips from the historic documentary The Last Pony Mine, filmed at the New Gladstone Mine near Centerville in 1971. The video concludes with the message that Iowa coal mining did not end because the coal was exhausted but because the high sulfur content of Iowa coal required additional processing, a time-consuming and costly process. From an economic point of view, Iowa coal cannot easily compete with low-sulfur coals. The walls of the theater are posted with maps of the underground coal mines of Des Moines. On these maps, two types of coal mines are easily distinguished. Room-and-pillar mines have a network pattern, while longwall mines have a

Subterranean Des Moines

Judging from present appearances, it's difficult to believe that Des Moines was once a bustling coal-mining town. But so it was. According to the Iowa Geological Survey there are 222 abandoned coal mines in the Des Moines area, 62 of which cannot be located because of incomplete records. Almost 20 square miles of the city are known to be undermined. Sometimes, the collapsing mines have caused the overlying ground surface to subside, causing sinkholes. The area east of the state capitol has been especially plagued with sinkholes.

Beginning in the 1840s, coal was quarried from outcrops along the riverbanks within the city. After the Civil War, the first major development of coal mining in Iowa took place in Des Moines when Wesley Redhead established the Des Moines Coal Company. Its best known mine, the Black Diamond (later renamed the Pioneer), was located south of the Raccoon River, near what is now the Seventh Street Bridge. The coal seam, 4.5 feet thick, was located 125 feet below the surface.

Overall, Polk County, of which Des Moines is the seat, is Iowa's second-leading coal-producing county, after top-ranked Monroe County. The county's peak annual coal production of two million tons came in 1917, when 3,000 miners were employed. Its last underground mine, near Urbandale, closed in 1947.

flowerlike shape, with fan-shaped petals of working faces radiating out in several directions from a central shaft.

The rest of the museum is enormous, and you can easily spend the whole day there. Near the entrance to the mine is an "economic minerals" exhibit, which contains samples of lead, limestone, gypsum, sand, and clay. A profile of the Tama Loam, Iowa's state soil, stands nearby. The "Ancient Life" exhibit contains fossil specimens of the scale tree (a coal producer), a huge slab of limestone covered with LeGrand starfish, and bones from mammoths that inhabited Iowa during the Ice Age.

Another exhibit related to the Iowa underground is located in the **Herrick Gallery** on the second floor. "The Urban Frontier" contains displays about pioneer life in Iowa's important towns. Of these, the Dubuque display features an eight-foot-high cave formation: a column produced by the fusion of a stalactite and a stalagmite. Samples of lead ore—shiny galena cubes—are also displayed.

The museum contains the important State Historical Society Library. Near the Locust Street entrance is an exhibit of Andrew Clemens's masterpiece of sand painting in a bottle, an equestrian portrait of George Washington, together with a collection of the artist's tools (see the sidebar for Sand Cave in Section I on page 92).

Directions: Adjacent to the state capitol building in downtown Des Moines.
Season/hours: Tuesday through Saturday, 9:00 a.m. to 4:30 p.m.; Sunday, noon to 4:30 p.m. Open on Mondays in the summer months (June through August). Free.
Length: 100 feet.
Precautions: None; it's wheelchair accessible.
Amenities: Terrace Café, gift shop, and superbly stocked bookstore.
Contact: State Historical Society of Iowa, 600 East Locust Street, Des Moines, IA 50319. Phone: (515) 281-5111. Web site: www.iowahistory.org

Ottumwa Coal Palace
Wapello County

THE FIRST BIG American industrial exposition was held in Philadelphia in 1876. Thereafter, individual states hosted their own expositions, with Iowa probably leading the nation in sheer numbers. Indeed, the late 1880s and early 1890s have been called Iowa's "Palace Age." During this period, several large exhibition halls were constructed, heavily decorated with the materials they were intended to promote. The five Corn Palaces of Sioux City began the tradition. Then there was the Blue Grass Palace in Creston, the Flax Palace in Forest City, the Hay Palace in Algona, the Ice Palace in Dubuque, and a proposed Onion Palace for Davenport. In Colfax, a million-dollar resort hotel was converted into the headquarters of the National Purebred Livestock Exchange and became known as the Great National Swine Palace, or, less gloriously, the Pig Palace. Ottumwa had its Coal Palace.

Ottumwa is the county seat of Wapello County, which saw its peak coal production in 1888. Two years later, Iowa's greatest monument to coal, the Ottumwa Coal Palace, was built. The Wapello County Historical Museum contains an elaborate scale model of the once-proud structure.

The entrance to the museum, where the offices of the Wapello County Historical Society are located, is on the second floor of

A model of the Ottumwa Coal Palace is the centerpiece of the Wapello County Historical Museum; the palace's creator, Peter Ballingall, peeks out from a stained-glass window behind the model.

Ottumwa's Amtrak station. You must take the elevator to get there, where your self-guided tour begins. You are welcomed by a likeness of "Mr. Ham," mascot of John Morrell & Company, the famous Ottumwa meat-packing company. Numerous exhibits deal with the history of the county in general, but underground enthusiasts will be awed by the model of the Ottumwa Coal Palace. The original structure formerly occupied what is now **Ballingall Park**, adjacent to the station.

In the late nineteenth century, Peter Ballingall, a Scottish immigrant, worked his way up from bellboy to owner of his own hotel—the Ballingall Hotel—and built the coal palace to promote the Iowa coal industry. All of the state's coal counties were invited to participate in the exhibit. The palace, a Gothic and Byzantine confection, was built in a former slough of the Des Moines River known as Sunken Park. It was 230 feet long, 130 feet wide, and included a central tower 200 feet high. True to its name, the "castle of jet" was veneered with glittering black coal and supported by pillars resembling coal shafts. Along its battlements, a frieze depicted Ottumwa's many industries, which indeed led to the town being dubbed the "Lowell of the West," after the industrial giant of Lowell, Massachusetts. The interior of the coal palace looked more like a corn palace, however, showcasing Iowa's agricultural products, including a huge corn mosaic portrait of Chief Wapello. It also contained a 35-foot-high re-creation of Niagara Falls. The palace opened on September 16, 1890, when ten thousand people jammed the building to hear President Benjamin Harrison give a speech.

The main attraction of the coal palace, however, was a coal mine replica under the building—which may perhaps be considered the forerunner of the coal mine replicas described in this book! Visitors were lowered down a shaft and boarded pit cars drawn by mules. Here, they could observe real miners at work with picks and shovels. Although coal was indeed mined within Ottumwa city limits, this particular mine was merely an imitation.

Public enthusiasm for the coal palace dwindled during its second season in 1891. Also that year, Ballingall passed away, and his funeral was held in the palace, which was demolished in 1892. Apart from deterioration of the external coal facings, the building posed an enormous fire hazard.

The museum's model of the Ottumwa Coal Palace was a labor of love for Milly Morris-Amos, who devoted a year and a half to constructing it. The model is large—six feet high, seven and a half feet long, and six feet wide—occupying an entire tabletop. The red-roofed model was pieced together from 6,000 pieces of blackboard slate, with coursings of real pea coal. The model, with its miniature stained glass windows, is surrounded by figurines engaged in a variety of activities. A mule is seen drawing a pit car of tourists out of the coal mine.

After examining the model of the coal palace, descend the stairway to the first floor of the museum, where another exhibit, "A Brief Summary of Coal Mining in Wapello County," can be found. Several coal-mining innovations originated in Ottumwa itself. The Ottumwa boxcar loader reduced coal breakage in the days when coal was carried in boxcars—not hoppers as it is today. The Hardsocg Manufacturing Company of Ottumwa manufactured the Little Wonder Drill, which is also included in the exhibit. This kind of rock drill was used to carve out the New York City subway system, Peruvian copper mines, and South African diamond mines. Other artifacts include a wooden coal car, carbide lamps, and various pieces of mining equipment.

Directions: Located in the Amtrak Depot on Main Street in downtown Ottumwa.

Season/hours: Tuesday through Saturday, 10:00 a.m. to 4:00 p.m.; closed on major holidays. Fee.

Precautions: None.

Amenities: Downtown Ottumwa.

Contact: Wapello County Historical Museum, 210 West Main Street, Ottumwa, IA 52501. Phone: (641) 682-8676.

Section III

Living Underground

IN THE FIRST two sections of this guidebook, we deal with "conventional" underground spaces: naturally occurring caves that are places to explore for recreation or geological interest; and mines from which valuable resources, such as lead and coal, were extracted. This section treats Iowa's underground as a space for living things.

These creatures include the bacteria and bugs that grow in the spaces between soil grains. We'll look at how crayfish, gophers, prairie dogs, and badgers excavate their own subterranean spaces in the soil, as shown so well in the Rootscape Tunnel and the Pecaut Artificial Loess Cave. Bats, the best known of cave inhabitants, can be seen at the Bat Cave in McGregor, in the Subterranean Biome at the Blank Park Zoo in Des Moines, or at the Putnam Museum in Davenport. Whole communities of organisms depend upon the microclimate created by ice caves, as on the algific talus slopes of northeastern Iowa, as seen at the University of Northern Iowa Museum in Cedar Falls.

Human beings, too, have sometimes chosen to lead a semisubterranean existence, as is evident in the Native American earth lodges found in western Iowa or suggested by the reproductions of prehistoric cave paintings on the walls of the Discovery Cave in the Battle Hill Museum. ■

45
Northeast Iowa Cold Air Community
Black Hawk County

THE GREEK word for cave, *spelunca*—from which words like spelunking and speleology are derived—carries the sense that caves are breathing places, the breathing holes of the Earth. This notion applies especially well to algific talus slopes, which you can learn about at the Northeast Iowa Cold Air Community exhibit at the **University of Northern Iowa Museum**.

If you've ever hiked the rugged landscape of northeast Iowa on muggy summer days, you probably already have an appreciation for "nature's air conditioning," the cold air that flows out of the spaces between loose stones (talus) on north-facing slopes. Some of that "refrigerated" air originates from hidden, inaccessible ice caves. What you may not have realized is that an entire living community, called

The algific slope diorama at the University of Northern Iowa Museum in Cedar Falls recreates a unique habitat related to hidden ice caves.

The Grinnell College Cave

It's fairly common to find cave or mine replicas at museums in Iowa and elsewhere, but at Iowa's Grinnell College, there used to be a man-made cave that recreated the exact climatic conditions inside a real cave.

Dr. Kenneth Christiansen, professor of biology at Grinnell, built the cave in 1961 with a National Science Foundation grant. Made of aluminum and steel and insulated with fiberglass, the cave was 10 feet by 10 feet and 8 feet high. An air conditioner maintained a temperature of 50 degrees Fahrenheit. Since over two hundred cave cultures from around the world were kept there, an alarm went off if the temperature strayed even a few degrees from the desired value.

Christiansen wanted to study the behavior, ecology, and evolution of cave-dwelling springtails—small, wingless insects about the size of a sesame seed; he is considered one of the world's leading experts on them. Most species live in the soil, where they are preadapted to cave life. The name "springtail" stems from an abdominal appendage that allows them to spring into the air. Christiansen, using springtails representing various stages of evolutionary development, observed how the insects moved over surfaces of various types. He found that the more cave-adapted species were able to walk on water, such as that found in cave pools, while less-adapted forms had not yet developed this ability.

Christiansen's experimental cave came to an untimely end after mites infested the structure. To eliminate them, he removed the cultures to a second, backup chamber while he disinfected the cave. Unfortunately, the backup didn't have a temperature alarm, and when the air conditioning failed, it killed all the cultures, destroying years of work. He lamented that it was "probably the worst moment of my scientific career."

Christiansen does recall lighter moments involving Grinnell's cave. In order to work comfortably in the dripping wet environment of the cave—necessary to maintain 99 percent humidity—he wore a heavy black raincoat and rubber boots. Suddenly opening the door of the cave one summer day, he startled a student nearby. "He bolted out like a frightened deer, never to be seen by me again," Christiansen chuckled. The cave was dismantled in 1989 when another faculty member took over the laboratory.

an algific slope community (algific means "cold producing"), depends on the cool, moist microclimate created by these drafts. Many species in these communities are otherwise only found farther north in Canada. According to the latest figures, there are more than three hundred significant algific talus slopes in the so-called Driftless Area of Iowa, Minnesota, Wisconsin, and Illinois; Iowa has a disproportionate share of these—approximately 240.

Algific talus slopes are not only cooler than their surroundings in summer, but warmer in winter. Their temperatures range from 50 degrees Fahrenheit in summer—a good average Iowa cave temperature—to 15 degrees in winter. This temperature range is considerably less than that of its surroundings.

Reversing air currents are responsible for this phenomenon. In summer, air is drawn into sinkholes, cools as it flows over subterranean ice, and escapes through vents onto the slopes. This ice deposit, remaining from the previous winter, is gradually melted by the currents of warmer air. Come winter again, the currents reverse. Air is sucked into the slope vents, refreezing the water and escaping up through sinkholes. This is also why a shale layer underlying the cavernous limestone is often considered a necessary ingredient for algific slopes—shale acts as a lower barrier for groundwater, allowing it to pool up and form ice.

With the proliferation of algific talus slopes in Iowa, it's no surprise that the state is home to an exhibit devoted to the subject. The University of Northern Iowa Museum features the splendid Algific Habitat Diorama, which shows a cross section of a shady limestone slope containing an ice cave. Depicted are loose limestone slabs covering the entrances to these voids and serving to diffuse the cold drafts across the slope. The diorama illustrates the diversity of living organisms found in algific environments. Plant life includes green hair moss, rose moss, tree apron moss, liverwort, walking fern, spinulosa wood fern, slender cliffbrake, bishop's cap, golden saxifrage, showy lady's slipper, currant, and yew. The algific slope trees featured include yellow birch, hornbeam, and black maple. Not shown in the diorama, but also frequently associated with algific slopes, are bald eagles, which nest on the cliffs above the slopes, and the slimy sculpin, a fish found in cold springs draining from the slopes.

By far the most famous resident of the algific slopes, however, is the Iowa Pleistocene snail (*Discus macclintocki*), an endangered species. This land snail is a quarter of an inch across—smaller than a shirt button—and feeds on the leaves of dead birch trees, a species not all that common in Iowa. Fossil shells of this snail, dating back to the Ice Ages, have long been known to specialists, but the snail was assumed to be extinct until living specimens were found in 1955 by biologist Leslie Hubricht. A separate display explains the snails.

Other exhibits in the museum deal with Iowa's underground sites. A panel is devoted to Coldwater Cave (see Section I), the largest cave in Iowa. Cave formations, such as stalactites, stalagmites, and helictites, and cave minerals, such as aragonite, are on display. A series of glass cases, each devoted to a separate geologic period, from the Precambrian to the present, contain examples of rocks, minerals, and fossils native to Iowa. There are also splendid dioramas of stuffed birds, African mammals, and anthropology displays.

In keeping with the algific, or "cold producing" theme, you should also visit the **Ice House Museum**, located at First and Clay Streets in downtown Cedar Falls. Built of hollow clay tile in 1921, this round structure, one hundred feet in diameter, was used to store ice harvested from the Cedar River, and is now on the National Register of Historic Places. Before the days of electricity, icemen carted the ice to residences throughout the city to fill iceboxes. Modern refrigeration and warmer winters forced the Ice House to close in 1934. The free museum is operated by the Cedar Falls Historical Society and contains displays about the local ice-harvesting industry and local history generally.

For additional references to algific talus slopes in this book, see the entries for Bat Cave, Bixby Ice Cave, Decorah Ice Cave, Malanaphy Springs, Old Brewery Art Gallery and Museum, and White Pine Hollow State Preserve.

Directions: On Hudson Road, just south of the UNI-Dome, on the University of Northern Iowa Campus in Cedar Falls.

Season/hours: Monday through Friday, 9:00 a.m. to 4:30 p.m.; weekends, 1:00 to 4:00 p.m.; closed holidays. Free.

Precautions: None.

Amenities: Gift shop.

Contact: University Museum, University of Northern Iowa, 3219 Hudson Road, Cedar Falls, IA 50614. Phone: (319) 273-2188. Web site: www.uni.edu/museum

46

Bat Caves
Clayton County

B AT CAVE is one of several types of caves in the McGregor area. When you think of "bat caves," you might think first of Batman and Robin's secret hideaway, but this one teems with genuine bats at certain times of the year. It's also easy to get to—just a mile north of McGregor on Highway 18 along the Mississippi River. Look for the McGregor District Office of the **Upper Mississippi River National Wildlife and Fish Refuge**. This huge tract was established in 1924 to protect the Mississippi flyway, where you can observe abundant waterfowl.

When you arrive at the office, go to the north end of the parking lot to the left of the entrance to the visitor center. There you will see a purple interpretive sign and the gated cave entrance in the sandstone bluff.

While you can't actually enter the bat cave, the gate allows you to get a good look at its interior; the wide spaces between the bars allow bats to fly through. If you want to see the bats, however, you need to visit the cave during hibernation season in winter, scanning especially the joints in the rock walls to find them. It is estimated that only about one cave in 50 makes a good bat cave, for various reasons. Certain birds also use this cave for nesting.

The bat cave is approximately 50 feet long and 12 feet wide and high, with a rounded vault. The herringbone pattern of pick marks on the sandstone walls indicates that the cave was hand dug. The Jordan Sandstone, named after rock exposures in Jordan, Minnesota, was deposited on tidal flats in the Cambrian seas. It is weakly cemented and friable—thus easily excavated.

The interpretive plaque states that the bat cave was originally the Hagensieck Brewery cave, dug in 1867. The cave was used to store ice and beer until the brewery closed in 1888, after which it was colonized by bats. Hundreds of bats used the cave until 1986, when it was sealed in the interest of public safety. Realizing how much bat habitat had been lost, officials reopened the cave in 1998. This episode illustrates how human activities have generally both helped and harmed bats. On one hand, the use of insecticides such as DDT has caused serious

The McGregor Bat Cave is a former brewery cave, dug long ago in the bluffs of the Mississippi River, that now serves as a bat hibernaculum.

declines in bat populations around the world. On the other hand, studies have shown that abandoned mines harbor far more bats than natural caves do in some parts of the world, including the Upper Midwest.

The plaque states that one bat can eat 1,200 insects per hour. (It should be pointed out, however, that contrary to folklore, bats don't usually eat all that many mosquitoes, preferring tastier fare such as moths.) Also, less than one-half of 1 percent of bats actually carries rabies. There are over nine hundred species of bats worldwide, of which 45 are found in the continental United States.

The visitor center, next to the bat cave, is well worth a visit, with displays on various underground phenomena. Algific talus slopes, which harbor unusual, cold-adapted plants and animals, are explained, as is a related geologic form, the maderate cliff, which is an algific slope that has lost its covering of stones by erosion. A three-dimensional cross section of an ice cave—accurate down to the imitation ice—is on display.

In addition to being the headquarters for the Upper Mississippi refuge, McGregor is also the headquarters of the **Driftless Area National Wildlife Refuge**, established in 1989 to protect eight hundred acres of algific slope habitat scattered among the 10,000 square miles of the Driftless Area in Iowa and surrounding states.

There are still more caves to see in McGregor—nicknamed the

"Pocket City" because it occupies a natural amphitheater in the bluffs. The town is well known for its man-made caves, which are most easily seen behind the buildings on Main Street near its intersection with A Street. Some of the cave entrances in the bluff are adjacent to the second story and are reached by a catwalk from the buildings. In the nineteenth century, these caves were used to store river ice and preserve perishable items. More recently, one of them was used by the Cave of the Elves gift shop.

There are also caves behind the **White Springs Supper Club**, on U.S. Highway 18 at the west side of McGregor. This restaurant is the site of the former Klein Brewery, which dug three beer caves in the Saint Peter sandstone. Located 30 feet below ground level, each one measured 25 feet wide, 60 feet long, and 7 feet high. Barrels of beer were slid down into the caverns and floated into place along a spring-fed trough system! These caves, still used for storage by the restaurant, are not accessible to the public, but you can peer into one of them from behind the counter.

Finally, you can explore several small, natural sandstone caves in neighboring Marquette. The caves are located in the outcrops along U.S. Highway 18, near the Isle of Capri Casino.

Directions:	Located on U.S. Highway 18, one mile north of downtown McGregor, along the Mississippi River.
Season/hours:	The bat cave display is accessible at any time. The Visitor Center hours are 8:00 a.m. to 4:30 p.m., Monday through Friday. Free.
Length:	50 feet.
Precautions:	None.
Amenities:	McGregor and Marquette are minutes away.
Contact:	McGregor District, P.O. Box 460, McGregor, IA 52157. Phone: (563) 873-3423.

47

Discovery Cave
Ida County

G ROPING YOUR WAY down a winding, darkened stairwell, you feel a draft of cold air and hear the sound of running water ahead. Your attention is drawn to the shadow of something along the walls—a rattlesnake, perhaps? Snakes often use caves for hibernation. Lucky for you, this one turns out to be a mounted specimen in a wall niche. Welcome to the Discovery Cave!

This cave is housed in the Battle Hill Museum of Natural History, established in 1990 and one of the "best-kept secrets" in northwestern Iowa. Battle Hill, the namesake of the museum, is a low mound about a mile east of town on the north side of State Highway 175, where a historical plaque commemorates an Indian battle in 1849. The museum is a favorite with local school groups and has been paid a special visit by the governor of the state. Three buildings and two floors groan under the weight of a well-organized natural history collection consisting of more than 4,000 specimens. The basement has been transformed into a cave. And it's all free!

Having passed through galleries filled with beautiful examples of the taxidermist's art, you arrive at the far end of the main building. The cave entrance is tucked away behind the towering skeleton of an African elephant.

At the bottom of the stairs you enter the cave proper. There are several grottoes in the cave, each illuminated with its own colored light—blue, green, or red. Stalactites, stalagmites, and columns—all artificial—decorate the cave. Stuffed bats hang from the ceiling. A waterfall adds realistic auditory effects. The temperature and humidity of the air simulate the actual conditions in a cave, so you might want a sweater if you stay a while, though 10 minutes would suffice for the whole experience.

You are free to move about the basement, but you must stay behind a railing on which educational information has been posted. As you turn to go back upstairs, images of Ice Age mammals catch your eye in the dim, half-light; they are reproductions of prehistoric cave paintings found in France!

Discovery Cave was not the first artificial cave in the museum's basement. In 1992, the director, Dennis Laughlin, constructed an elaborate cave from lumber and sheetrock. A map of this original cave, posted on the museum walls, resembles a complicated newspaper pencil maze. One day, exhausted after leading several hundred visitors through this labyrinth with a flashlight, he decided to demolish it and build a self-guided cave. The new cave, finished in 1999, is the single, large, open chamber you see today. Laughlin molded chicken wire over the basement walls, floor, ceiling, and support beams, covered it with aluminum foil, and sprayed foam insulation over the whole thing, creating a very believable cave landscape. By using spray foam, he designed to imitate "popcorn texture,"

The basement of the Battle Hill Museum of Natural History has been converted into the rainbow-hued Discovery Cave, complete with a waterfall.

a natural roughness of cave walls. On the wall next to the cave entrance are photographs showing stages in the construction of this new cave. Discovery Cave is meant to represent a limestone cave, the sort associated with eastern Iowa; in this part of Iowa, "caves" are more often associated with man-made excavations in the wind-deposited loess soils.

Seeing the rest of the museum will take much more time, so budget a couple of hours to take it all in. The six hundred wildlife mounts, not confined to local fauna, include large animals such as tigers and giraffes, whose bodies were obtained from a nearby zoo. There are 70 head mounts and 200 antlers. One glass case is chock full of bison skulls collected from the alluvium of the Soldier River. The Van Wyngarden Wildfowl Collection consists of 375 bird mounts, some dating back to 1914, tastefully arranged in a single room. The room devoted to seashells includes a 545-pound giant clam. Despite its reputation, this "man-eating" clam fed only on microscopic organisms. Rocks, minerals, and fossils round out the collection.

Another outstanding natural history museum in this part of Iowa is the **Sanford Museum** in Cherokee, which had the first planetarium in the state. The town of Cherokee became famous in the 1880s for the most unusual spa in Iowa, based on supposedly magnetic groundwater. A splendid hotel called the Fountain House and a horse-racing track were constructed at the spa, but nothing now remains of it.

Directions: The museum is located on the northeast corner of the intersection of State Highway 175 and Chestnut Street in Battle Creek. Look for the name of the museum painted on the side of the white buildings. There are gravel parking lots at the front and sides of the museum.

Season/hours: The first Sunday of June, July, and August, 1:00 to 5:00 p.m.; any time by appointment. Free, donations appreciated.

Precautions: The tour is self-guided and does not require a flashlight.

Amenities: A small gift shop.

Contact: Battle Hill Museum of Natural History, State Highway 175 East, Battle Creek, IA 51006. Phone: (712) 365-4414. Web site: www.pionet.net/~bhmuseum

48

Rootscape Tunnel
Jasper County

THE ROOTSCAPE TUNNEL in the Prairie Learning Center of the Neal Smith National Wildlife Refuge is conceptually unique among the exhibits described in this guide in its approach to providing a subterranean experience. The word cave usually connotes the idea that the underground space it refers to is large enough for human beings to enter. The Rootscape requires a mental flip-flop. Here, you are asked to imagine yourself shrunk down to the size of an insect so that your surroundings are much larger than they normally seem. For example, soil pores appear to be caves and roots are trunk-sized. According to a curator, children implicitly get the idea, whereas adults often have to have it all explained to them! In this regard, the Rootscape bears a certain resemblance to the Underground Adventure exhibit at the well-known Field Museum of Natural History in Chicago.

Upon descending the ramp into the Rootscape you see a banner overhead with the words "Most of Prairie Life is Underground." That's a surprising statement, especially if you've heard the stories about mounted horsemen riding through prairie grass so tall they couldn't see over it and about the enormous herds of bison that used to roam the prairies. Under the banner, however, is a square pillar of soil that shows the diversity of living organisms beneath the prairie—especially the extensive root systems of prairie plants. An imitation bullsnake coils in its burrow, several feet below the surface. To the right of the entrance to the Rootscape is a display entitled "Much More Than Dirt," showing a complex soil community. Historically, the first person to dramatize what prairies look like underground was J. E. Weaver of the University of Nebraska, in the 1930s. The Dust Bowl had laid bare the destructive agricultural practices of the time. Weaver, by digging trenches, demonstrated how deep-rooted native prairie vegetation is better able to cope with dry spells than are mankind's less-well-adapted crop plants.

The Rootscape itself is a tunnel about 50 feet long, its interior lined with shotcrete (sprayed concrete) painted chocolate brown. The main feature is the Kid's Maze, which adults can easily navigate without

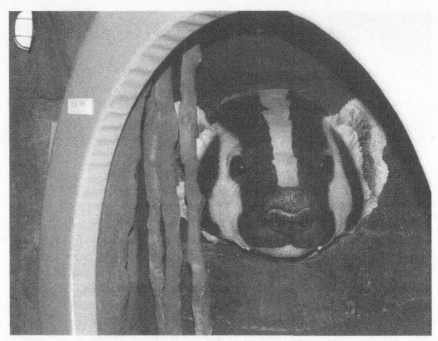

A whale-sized badger greets visitors to the Neal Smith Rootscape Tunnel.

even stooping. "Inside this maze," a sign announces, "your kids can be tiny bugs crawling around prairie roots." You step through the arch and are confronted by a snarling badger head—the size of a whale's head—staring at you. Make your way among the roots of the prairie plants, which at this scale seem like pillars.

A display invites you to push a button to take an X-ray of tallgrass prairie sod. Doing so, and squinting in the eerie, bluish light, you glimpse the skeleton of a gopher among the root tangles. Pocket gophers loosen the soil and create underground pantries, which help recycle nutrients downward.

Leaving the far end of the Rootscape Tunnel, you wend your way among the prairie displays in the 13,000-square-foot exhibit hall. One display features the prairie crayfish, a creature that creates entrances to its burrows that look like miniature volcanoes. Unlike most crayfish, this one can actually live on land if it's wet enough. This display, like others, again emphasizes the concept that some animals can only exist on the prairie by going underground. Other displays in the Prairie Learning Center cover the history of the Iowa prairies.

The Tallgrass Trail, north of the center, leads you on a two-mile paved walking loop through a prairie. The Savanna Trail, east of the center, winds through an oak-hickory savanna. Trail brochures point out that the Indiana bat, an endangered species, roosts in the hollows of prairie trees such as the bur oak and under the loose bark of shagbark hickories. Each spring, pregnant female bats return to this wildlife refuge from their wintering caves in Missouri.

The Neal Smith National Wildlife Refuge was established in 1990 on the former proposed site of a nuclear power plant. The refuge protects 5,000 acres of tallgrass prairie, an achievement that pays tribute to Iowa's original landscape. Only one-tenth of 1 percent of the original tallgrass prairie that covered 85 percent of the state is left. The refuge was dedicated by former congressman Neal Smith and Vice President Al Gore.

Directions: From State Highway 163, 20 miles east of Des Moines, take Exit 18 at Prairie City. Follow the signs along the long, winding access road (Pacific Street).

Season/hours: The Prairie Learning Center is open Tuesday through Saturday from 9:00 a.m. to 4:00 p.m. and Sunday from noon to 5:00 p.m. The auto tour route and walking trails are open during daylight hours. Free.

Length: 50 feet.

Precautions: None. It's wheelchair accessible.

Amenities: Prairie Point Bookstore.

Contact: Neal Smith NWR, Box 399, Prairie City, IA 50228. Phone: (515) 994-3400. Phone: (515) 994-3400. Web site: www.tallgrass.org

49
Earth Lodges
Mills County

For centuries, earth lodges—which resemble grass-covered igloos from a distance—were widely used as dwellings among Native Americans in the Missouri River basin. As with the sod huts of early white settlers, the soil of the semisubterranean lodges insulated them from excessive heat or cold. In late prehistoric times, the earth lodge idea—characteristic of the Plains—migrated eastward from Platte River country and took root in the vicinity of what later became the town of Glenwood in southwestern Iowa. The Glenwood culture flourished from 1150 to 1300 A.D. Archaeologically speaking, Iowa is situated along the border between the Plains cultures of the West and the Woodland cultures of the East.

An earth lodge, of the type used by early Native American inhabitants of western Iowa, is located in Glenwood. Photo by Cindy Doty.

The Mound-Builder Controversy

As settlers streamed west into the Ohio and Mississippi River valleys after the Revolutionary War they encountered vast numbers of earthen mounds. There were an estimated 100,000 mounds in eastern North America—10,000 in Iowa alone. They were so plentiful in the state that the Des Moines River was known as the River of the Mounds. Even though the mounds were built by Native Americans, most nineteenth-century archeologists attributed their construction to a vanished race of superior beings unrelated to the natives.

Amateur archeologists in Iowa and elsewhere were keen to dig the mounds for buried treasure. Some of the finds included copper artifacts, galena cubes, sheets of mica, freshwater pearls, and pottery. The Mound Builders were inveterate smokers, judging from the huge numbers of pipes found. Rectangular crypts made of logs containing human skeletons were also found, along with what appeared to be sacrificial altars.

The mounds are divisible into at least three kinds: conical burial mounds, effigy mounds—low, animal-shaped mounds that did not contain burials—and earthworks. Each kind is characteristic of a certain area. Earthworks found in the Ohio Valley were regarded as a sort of prehistoric version of France's Maginot Line, constructed by the Mound Builders to hold back some vague enemy—presumably, the ancestors of the present Native Americans. It was argued that the labor involved in such enormous earth-moving projects required a steady food supply such as only a corn-based agriculture could supply.

Despite the insistence that the Mound Builders were unrelated to Native Americans, there were always some who surmised the truth. Some observed that man-made mounds were actually a worldwide phenomenon, with many cultures exhibiting a mound-building phase. It was pointed out that Lewis and Clark observed a mound being erected over the body of a Native American chief. But it was not until Cyrus Thomas, working for the then recently founded U.S. Bureau of Ethnology, published his massive report in 1894 that the Mound-Builder myth was finally demolished. He concluded that mound builders were actually the ancestors of the present Native Americans, not a vanished race of superior beings.

While you can see mounds in many parks in eastern Iowa, the best place in the state is the spectacular **Effigy Mounds National Monument** near Harpers Ferry, (563) 873-3491.

While no earth lodges have survived intact, remnants are common in the Keg and Pony Creek drainages in western Mills County. Altogether, some 240 lodges have been documented thus far, a mere fraction of the original number. In 1992, the Earth Lodge Society, using modern earth-moving machinery, re-created one of these dwellings in Glenwood Lake Park. Vegetation soon established itself in the soil on top of the lodge. Experience for yourself what it was like to live underground in Iowa almost a thousand years ago!

The replica represents a typical Glenwood earth lodge, square in shape, about 30 feet on each side with rounded corners. The lodge dweller entered through a covered passage that was oriented south to avoid prevailing winds. The lodges were built in shallow depressions and the walls consisted of closely set vertical poles. There were four main roof supports located in the center of the lodge around the central fire pit. Clay plaster was used to prevent water leakage and to protect the wood inside the lodge from catching fire. The floor of the lodge was pockmarked with holes—the openings to cache pits where corn and other foodstuffs could be stored.

The Mill Creek culture of northwestern Iowa, contemporary with the Glenwood, also constructed earth lodges, but they were elongated rather than square and were concentrated into palisaded villages rather than being scattered in isolated locations along streams in the Loess Hills.

By the time Lewis and Clark made their way up the Missouri River in 1804, the Glenwood people had vanished. Whether they had moved away or simply blended with other peoples is uncertain. The tradition of building earth lodges, which died out in Iowa, continued for a time in other parts of the Great Plains. Fort Lincoln State Park in North Dakota, for example, has reconstructed earth lodges from a more recent Mandan Indian village. The Field Museum of Natural History in Chicago has a large indoor model of a Pawnee earth lodge from the Platte River of Nebraska.

The Glenwood earth lodge replica is located just across the street from the **Mills County Historical Museum**, from which the lodge tours depart. The museum contains a painting entitled "Earth Lodge Country in Winter" that emphasizes once again why native peoples chose to live in such well-insulated structures—to protect themselves from the brutal winters of the Plains. It's interesting to note that more archaeological research has been conducted in Mills County than in any other Iowa county, and the museum reflects that emphasis. It contains the Rowe Collection, one of the best archaeological collections focusing on the central part of the Missouri River valley. A huge number of arrowheads adorns the walls. Paul Rowe (1894–1968) was an avid amateur archaeologist to whom we are indebted for much of our knowledge of this area.

The archaeologist Ellison Orr, director of the 1938 Mills County Survey for the Works Progress Administration, excavated many of the lodges, and the museum has photographs of this work. A rather unusual aspect of these lodge excavations is that many of the sites were located on the grounds of the Glenwood State Hospital-School (formerly the Institution for the Feeble-Minded). During the 1930s and 1940s, the inmates made a hobby of excavating the lodges. While their digging techniques were said to have been sloppy even by the standards of the day, they were generous in sharing whatever they did find.

Directions: The earth lodge is located on the north side of U.S. Highway 34 (Sharp Street) in Glenwood. Park at the Mills County Museum (from which tours depart), located in Glenwood Lake Park, just across from the earth lodge.

Season/hours: By appointment only. The museum is open on weekends, 1:30 to 4:00 p.m., Memorial Day to Labor Day, and by appointment. Fee.

Length: 20 feet.

Precautions: None.

Amenities: Glenwood Lake Park has picnic tables, pavilions, playgrounds, camping, and the Davies Amphitheater. The town of Glenwood is minutes away.

Contact: Mills County Historical Museum, Glenwood Lake Park, Highway 34 E, Glenwood, IA 51534. Phone: (712) 537-5038.

Subterranean Biome
Polk County

D ES MOINES has several interesting caves, but you'll have to go to the Blank Park Zoo to see them. Your journey begins at the zoo's Discovery Center. Enter by way of a re-created Alpine cabin and follow the rushing mountain stream down to the warmer climates beyond. The first cavelike space you come to features an enclosure containing the Madagascar hissing cockroach, which can grow up to four inches long. The roach hisses by expelling air from holes in the side of its body, called spiracles, which it does when handled, fighting, or courting. The emperor scorpion from Africa, among the largest of all scorpions, glows brilliant blue under black light in a nearby enclosure. The floor of the cave is transparent, allowing you to see uncomfortably well into a live snake pit directly

The only cave in Des Moines, in the subterranean biome at the Blank Park Zoo, contains live specimens of the Egyptian fruit bat.

Cave Biology

The study of cave biology in the United States began at Mammoth Cave, Kentucky, in the nineteenth century. Cave animals, or cavernicoles, are often divided into four groups. Troglobites (cave dwellers) can live only in caves. They are the "classic" cave organisms, the ones associated with loss of eyes and pigmentation, feeding on organic matter brought in by floods—or on each other. Troglophiles (cave lovers) prefer caves but are not specially cave adapted. The so-called freshwater shrimp (also known as amphipods, or scuds) found at most springs in Iowa cave country is considered a troglophile. Trogloxenes (cave strangers) use caves for daily or seasonal shelter. Almost anyone who has entered a cave has been annoyed by mosquitoes and crane flies at the entrance, and these are examples of trogloxenes. Accidentals form the last group. If a pig inadvertently fell into a cave through a sinkhole—an occurrence that is featured in several cave-discovery narratives—the poor fellow would be considered an accidental!

Creatures that prefer caves are not scattered randomly through the animal kingdom. Certain groups predominate. There are more arthropods in caves (as on the surface) than all other groups combined. Among terrestrial arthropods, beetles dominate, while in aquatic settings, crustaceans do. In 1990, researchers Stewart Peck and Kenneth Christiansen published a now-classic survey of cave invertebrates that included Iowa. Other invertebrates found in Iowa caves included flatworms, earthworms, snails, isopods, spiders, mites, centipedes, and millipedes. Christiansen, a world-renowned expert on springtails, is based at Grinnell College in Iowa.

One of Iowa's most bizarre cave dwellers is a ghostly white amphipod known as Stygobromus. It is a relict species found in only a few Iowa caves, separated by a considerable distance from the rest of its kin elsewhere in the United States. It is thought that the surface-dwelling ancestor of this crustacean had a continuous distribution across the whole area before the Ice Ages. Caves provided a refuge beneath the ice-covered land surface.

Among the vertebrates, blind cavefish, which abound in Missouri, are not known in Iowa caves, although Muenster Cave in Dubuque was once rumored to harbor them. Some salamanders inhabit caves. Ironically, the best-known cave animal, the bat, is classified as a trogloxene, or cave stranger, because bats neither feed in caves nor complete their life cycle there. The eleven species of bats in Iowa may be divided into tree bats, which are solitary and migrate south for the winter, and cave bats, which are colonial and usually hibernate in caves or mines during the winter.

Even cave bats, however, must make at least a short autumn migration to get to the cave they will inhabit for the winter. In spring, the bats disperse from the caves and roost in woodlands or buildings. The bat that supposedly eats mosquitoes is the little brown; the most common house bat is the big brown. The eastern pipistrelle prefers moister situations; it is found in stream caves and in chinks in the walls of storm sewers. Paradoxically, the larger the cluster that a species of bat forms in a cave, the rarer that species is likely to be since it becomes more vulnerable to disturbance once that particular spot is wiped out. Such is the case for the Indiana bat, which is the only federally endangered mammal in Iowa.

below. Continue through the butterfly garden and around a waterfall to the main attraction, the Subterranean Biome.

The biome, an artificial bat cave, is the only exhibit of its kind in Iowa. Here, you stand among stalactites, stalagmites, and columns and peer into a ghostly landscape diorama. Live Egyptian fruit bats (*Rousettus aegyptiacus*) with wingspans up to two feet fly around in the artificial moonlight inside the diorama. They are nocturnal and use echolocation to navigate. They are found well beyond Egypt, existing in Turkey, Cyprus, Pakistan, Arabia, and in most of Africa south of the Sahara. They roost in ancient tombs and temples, date plantations, but usually in caves. By sipping nectar from flowers, they act as pollinators.

If you leave the bat cave at the right moment you may be startled by a clap of thunder and a sudden rain shower—you have reached a lush re-creation of the Amazon River along with its inhabitants. For the children, there is another underground experience ahead. Outside, where you can see more than eight hundred animals from five continents, there is a prairie dog exhibit where kids can crawl on their hands and knees through a rubber-padded concrete pipe 20 feet long to reach a viewing station in the center of a prairie dog town.

Directions: Blank Park Zoo is located on the south side of Des Moines near the international airport. From State Highway 5, take Exit 96 and head north on 9th Street SW; the zoo is on your right.

Season/hours: Daily, 10:00 a.m. to 5:00 p.m.; 10:00 a.m. to 7:00 p.m. Fridays (May through August). Fee.

Length: 50 feet.

Precautions: None. It's wheelchair accessible.

Amenities: Gift shop, River Bank Café.

Contact: Blank Park Zoo, 7401 SW 9th Street, Des Moines, IA 50315. Phone: (515) 285-4722. Web site: www.blankparkzoo.com

51

Secrets of the Cave
Scott County

MAQUOKETA CAVES State Park (see section I) has been re-created at the **Putnam Museum** in Davenport. Established in 1867, the Putnam is the third-oldest museum west of the Mississippi River. A relatively new exhibit, "Black Earth/Big River," provides you with a look at past and present natural habitats of the Quad Cities region, of which Davenport is a part. The most unique feature of this new exhibit is "Secrets of the Cave," a winding cave passage.

A cougar on the rocks above you guards the entrance to this lighted, wheelchair-accessible cave. Just inside the entrance is a diorama of a Devonian coral reef, reflecting the origin of the local bedrock. As with real caves, as you go deeper into this one you encounter zones of successively more cave-adapted inhabitants. Near the entrance is a display of animals that use the cave for temporary shelter. Called "Out of the Weather," it displays bones left by an animal that used the cave. A glass case features cave minerals and formations. You then come to "Snakes Alive, A Winter Hibernaculum," showing a simulated knot of blue racers and fox snakes.

Going deeper into the cave, you come to another re-creation, a cluster of endangered Indiana bats, the rarest bat in Iowa. On the opposite wall is an informational sign entitled "Drip, Drip, Drip," explaining how caves form. You learn that limestone caves are often formed by a chemical solution, whereas sandstone caves—as at nearby Wildcat Den State Park (see section I)—are often created by the mechanical erosion of rocks by flowing water. Then, you encounter various cave formations, such as stalactites, stalagmites, and columns. Water ripples over imitation flowstone. These formations recall the ones found in the Steel Gate Passage of Dancehall Cave in Maquoketa Caves State Park.

No pains were spared to achieve an accurate representation. The 40-foot cave, constructed of shotcrete (sprayed concrete), took nine months to build, and it was difficult to recapture the right yellowish-brown textures seen in the real Maquoketa caves. A lot of effort was

The Putnam Museum in Davenport features a meticulously reconstructed cave passage from Maquoketa Caves State Park.

spent just on getting the bat guano to look real; it was convincing enough for me!

Emerging from the other end of the cave—this time guarded by a coyote—you arrive at "The Black Earth," an interactive display involving Iowa soils. According to the exhibit, a one-inch thickness of prairie soil can take four hundred years to form. The bushy roots of big bluestem grass, carefully dug from the soil near Muscatine, are displayed. "Aerating the Soil" presents a cutaway view of a badger burrow. A water-well display explains why wells should be properly sealed if they are no longer in use: they can act as conduits for contamination.

Other parts of the "Black Earth/Big River" exhibit have subterranean associations. You are invited to balance the weight of a little brown bat against the number of insects you think it would consume in a night (a thousand or so). A video kiosk with brief clips, one of them entitled Visiting Bat Caves, shows a trip to a lead mine near Savanna, Illinois, while another has instructions on building backyard bat houses.

The Putnam Museum has many other exhibits, such as "River, Prairie, and People: The Heritage of the Quad Cities Region," a historical panorama of the Quad Cities from the retreat of the glaciers to local jazz musician Bix Beiderbecke. The museum also displays fake artifacts used in the Davenport Conspiracy of the late nineteenth century, a bizarre archaeological hoax that included a phony "zodiac" carved on slate that was planted in a local Indian mound to intentionally dupe researchers (see the sidebar "The Mound-Builder Controversy" on page 167).

Directions: The Putnam Museum is located in Fejervary Park in downtown Davenport; follow the signs.

Season/hours: Monday through 9:00 a.m. to 5:00 p.m.; Saturday, 10:00 a.m. to 5:00 p.m.; Sunday, noon to 5:00 p.m. Fee.

Length: 40 feet.

Precautions: None. It's wheelchair accessible.

Amenities: Gift shop, River Bank Café.

Contact: Putnam Museum, 1717 West 12th Street, Davenport, IA 52804. Phone: (800) 435-3701. Web site: www.putnam.org

52
Artificial Loess Cave
Woodbury County

T HE DUST BOWL of the 1930s wasn't the first one to hit the
United States, nor was it the largest. During the waning of the
last Ice Age, there was a "dust bowl" so great that the falling
dust formed a range of hills that resemble gigantic snowdrifts. The
Loess Hills of western Iowa are the result.

The current explanation, however, took a long time to be accepted.
One early theory held that the material making up the Loess Hills
originated as meteoritic dust from outer space! Finally, an Iowa sci-
entist, Bohumil Shimek (commemorated in Shimek State Forest in
southeastern Iowa), solved the mystery. He concluded that the dust
was actually rock flour that was produced by glaciers grinding over
bedrock during the Ice Ages. Washed out from under the glaciers by
streams of meltwater, the silt was deposited nearby, dried out, and
then swept aloft by prevailing winds. Loess is also prominent in the
Rhine Valley of Germany (where the word, pronounced "luss," originally came from) and, on a truly monumental scale, in China.

The Dorothy Pecaut Nature Center just north of Sioux City contains an artificial loess cave, which is about as close as most people
will get to going underground in the Loess Hills. Prairie grasses and
flowers adorn the ground surface above the cave, which is about
20 feet long. Inside, the roots of those same grasses, represented by
twine, dangle down upon your head. You learn that twice as much
plant material is located below the surface of a prairie as above. The
gray color of the walls represents unweathered loess, which hasn't
been oxidized. Oxidation would turn it yellow or brown.

Once inside the loess cave, peer into the "Underground Nursery," a
small den containing a stuffed badger, and look out through a hole to
the surface, where another badger peers back in at you. Badgers dig
burrows like this to escape the heat and dryness of the surface.

The loess cave is only one of many things to see and do at the
nature center. One of the most interesting displays is "Children of the
Loess," which explains the fortuitously human-shaped concretions
(kindchen, in German) found in the loess. Concretions are hard,
compact accumulations of mineral matter that grow inside soils or

The Dorothy Pecaut Nature Center, near Sioux City, contains an artificial loess cave that shows the geological composition of the nearby Loess Hills.

other rocks. A glass case displays items relating to the founding of **Stone State Park**, which surrounds the center. In 1885, the eccentric naturalist Daniel Hector Talbot began raising exotic animals here. In 1895, Thomas Jefferson Stone acquired the Talbot farm, and his son, Edgar, began developing it as a park. Sioux City acquired the Stone property for a city park, and in 1935 it became a state park. Outcrops of the underlying Cretaceous-age bedrock—not usually visible in the Loess Hills—are found here, so the park lives up to the word stone in another sense! Stone State Park is but one stop on the 220-mile **Loess Hills National Scenic Byway**, which parallels the western border of Iowa.

Directions: From Interstate 29 in Sioux City, take Exit 151 and follow State Highway 12 (Sioux River Road) north four miles, passing through the town of Riverside. Watch for Stone State Park and the sign indicating the nature center, reached by a long driveway leading uphill into the parking lot. There is no automobile access to the nature center from within the state park itself.

Season/hours: Tuesday through Saturday, 9:00 a.m. to 5:00 p.m., Sunday, 1:00 to 5:00 p.m., year round; Tuesday, Thursday, 9:00 a.m. to 8:00 p.m., May through October. Free.

Length: 20 feet.

Precautions: None. It's wheelchair accessible.

Amenities: The center has a bookstore and the Terra Resource Room, a library of field guides and audiovisual materials. Picnic tables, hiking trails.

Contact: Woodbury County Conservation Board, Dorothy Pecaut Nature Center, 4500 Sioux River Road, Sioux City, IA 51109. Phone: (712) 258-0838. Web site: www.woodburyparks.com

Other Sites

Section IV
Other Sites

HUMAN BEINGS interact with the underground in many ways other than cave exploration and mining; this section will explore some of them. Iowa has its own unique set of geological circumstances, which gives rise to a unique combination of underground sites. Because of its comparative flatness, for example, the state does not have many tunnels, even though it has one of the most extensive "Rails to Trails" programs in the United States—a program that has freed up many railroad tunnels and tracks for public access in other states. Iowa's one vehicular tunnel—for automobiles— was originally a mill tunnel. Having a historical tendency toward Prohibition, Iowa is not especially rich in brewery caves or underground wine cellars either, but there are a few. And while Iowa once had true underground spaces on its own stretch of the Underground Railroad (see the sidebar "Iowa's Underground Railroad" on page 184), these have not been maintained, as they have elsewhere.

On the other hand, as home to the Grotto of the Redemption, Iowa was the cradle of the religious grotto-building movement that swept the Midwest, and it continues to be innovative in this field, as may be seen in the "secular" grotto created by the Life Engineering Foundation at Bridgewater. Most unusual of all, Iowa has the Bertrand, a steamboat that lay hidden under the prairie like a time capsule from a bygone era. These are just a few of the attractions we'll visit in this section. ■

53

EOWATA
Adair County

W HERE IN IOWA can you take a journey to the center of the Earth? In the caves of EOWATA, a facility operated by the Life Engineering Foundation.

The foundation's creator, Jack Ench, graduated from the Rolla School of Mines in Missouri and served with the Atomic Energy Commission. In 1960 he stated that he had a visionary experience in which he beheld what would later become Camp Eo–Wa–Ta, now EOWATA. Ten years later, he began building the 88-acre retreat amid the rolling farmland of southern Iowa. Here, he taught a holistic life philosophy that is introduced in his book, *Life and Consciousness*. To aid in conceptualizing the teachings of modern science, he constructed a walk-through model of a star and a landscape representing the surface of the Earth three billion years ago, including three kinds of caves.

The three-hour tour, which includes a free meal when tickets are reserved at least 24 hours in advance, begins at the main office where tickets can be purchased. The tour, referred to as a "play," is divided into three parts, or "acts," each covering a theme in the 15-billion-year history of our universe. You are taken by trolley to Act One, which represents the universe before the formation of the Earth. Here, the main attraction is a walk-through star and an observatory.

Act Two, which tells the story of the Earth before life began, involves an underground experience. You walk out onto a one-acre shotcrete landscape featuring a giant replica of planet Earth, Wyoming's Devil's Tower, the Old Faithful geyser, a natural bridge, and erosional landforms known as "hoodoos."

The underground tour begins when you enter an artificial limestone cave, again made from shotcrete, complete with stalagmites, stalactites, columns, and a stream. Your guide explains how caves are formed. The humidity and cool temperatures evoke the conditions inside a real cave and, on hot days, are a delicious relief from the heat. The lighting is kept to a minimum to maintain the effect as you grope your way through a narrow, dark passage until you reach a stairway of cement blocks. People who are unsure of their footing should not

At EOWATA, visitors enter a volcano and take a journey to the center of the earth at the headquarters of the Life Engineering Foundation in Bridgewater.

proceed beyond this point even though there is a railing because the treads of the stairway are narrow and the risers high.

At the top of the stairs, you enter a large dome, 40 feet in diameter. Congratulations, you have just completed a "Journey to the Center of the Earth"! You are now inside the replica of planet Earth that you saw from the outside. The dome is eerily illuminated by a red sphere 10 feet in diameter at the center—the glowing core! Watch where you walk because you don't want to step in the bubbling pools of "magma" (actually, water illuminated with red light). Your guide explains the Earth's anatomy.

Going back downstairs, you walk through a model of a volcano. The rim of the crater is represented by a skylight high above you. The guide points out a "gold mine"—glittering spangles running in veins through the wall. You are also shown a "crystal cave" containing amethysts. You walk through a lava tube cave, past a waterfall, and back to the outside world. Notice that lava tube caves have stalagmites and stalactites just like limestone caves, except that they are drip forms created by congealed lava, rather than by precipitated calcite.

The water from the artificial waterfalls and geysers of this reconstructed landscape ultimately drains over a miniature Niagara Falls into a quiet pond whose floating mats of algae are used to suggest the primordial soup from which life began.

The tour continues to Act Three, which you reach by riding a replica of the steamboat Clermont up a canal back to the main grounds. Robert Fulton constructed the Clermont, an early steamboat, on the Hudson River in New York in 1807. Act Three demonstrates the appearance of life on Earth; it includes a tour of the beautifully landscaped flower gardens and fountains of the main grounds. The tour ends at Fleet's Hall, where guests can get an introduction to the philosophy presented by the Life Engineering Foundation.

Directions: Two miles east of Bridgewater on State Highway 92 is Delta Avenue and a sign referring to the Life Engineering Foundation. Head south on Delta Avenue, a gravel road, for three miles. The road veers in several places, but keep going; when you pass the Witt Cemetery on the right, you are almost there. Just beyond, on the right side, is the rainbow-arch entrance to EOWATA. Park in the gravel lot on the opposite side of the road. Walk through the arch and grounds to the office.

Season/hours: Memorial Day to Labor Day. Tours start at 10:00 a.m., noon, and 5:00 p.m. daily, except Tuesday and Thursday. The tour lasts two to three hours. Fee; includes a free meal when tickets are reserved at least 24 hours in advance.

Precautions: Some of the caves are wet. One staircase along the tour is short but steep.

Amenities: Souvenir shop. EOWATA offers a 26-room guest lodge, dining hall, and classrooms for those taking courses at the Life Engineering Foundation.

Contact: Life Engineering Foundation, 2953 Delta Avenue, Bridgewater, IA 50837. Phone: (800) 852-5072 or (641) 369-2391. Web site: www.lifeengineering.org

54

Herbert Hoover
Library and Museum
Cedar County

NOT MANY people are aware that before he became the nation's president, Herbert Hoover—the only Iowa native to achieve that distinction—was a world-famous mining engineer. The Herbert Hoover Library and Museum in West Branch, where he was born in 1874, devotes ample space to this aspect of his multifaceted career.

To gain perspective of his achievements, you begin by watching a 22-minute biographical overview of Hoover's life. Pass through the rotunda, with its 16-foot red granite map of the world, and take a winding stroll through the museum galleries, where the biographical exhibits are arranged chronologically. First you see a statue of Hoover as a boy fishing in the West Branch creek. Following is a corrugated shed, containing a carbide lamp, and a life-size plaster model of the young man sitting at a table examining ore specimens while smoking a pipe. In the background you see an Australian gold mine. Hoover, who was one of the first students at the newly established Stanford University, worked in the California gold mines after graduation. He traveled through Western Australia on a camel, visiting Coolgardie, Kalgoorlie, and Leonora, inspecting gold mines on behalf of the London firm of Bewick, Moreing and Company. He concluded that gold mining was the least profitable aspect of the business and that large bodies of low-grade ore offered the best chance of success.

Hoover's next assignment was to manage a coal and cement company in China and serve as director of a state-owned mine; at the time foreigners were snatching up mining concessions in China's enormously coal-rich regions. The Chinese peasants held Hoover in awe, regarding him as the "great foreign mandarin" who could "see through the ground to find gold." But he was caught in the siege of Tianjin during the Boxer Rebellion of 1900, when Westerners were attacked. In one of the museum displays, a plaster model of his wife Lou, undaunted, stands ready with a cannon.

Iowa's Underground Railroad

The Underground Railroad was a system for helping fugitive slaves from the South escape to free northern states and Canada. It began operation after the War of 1812—in the days before actual railroads—and lasted until the Civil War. It eventually had "agents," "conductors," and "stations," and sometimes involved actual travel by rail. But the term "underground" was more suggestive of the secrecy involved than a physical location below ground. Under the cover of darkness, fugitive slaves were transported from one "station" (often a private home) to the next and were commonly hidden during the day in cellars and attics until the next night's move.

There were two main routes through Iowa, the eastern and the western. The eastern route ran through Salem, the first Quaker settlement west of the Mississippi River. Many residents of the town aided fugitive slaves from the adjoining state of Missouri, which practiced slavery. The western route ran through the town of Tabor and is associated with the famous abolitionist John Brown, who later raided the federal arsenal at Harper's Ferry, Virginia (now West Virginia), a deed for which he was hanged. Tabor supplied arms to the Kansas Territory, where there was conflict between abolitionists and proslavery forces.

None of the routes ran north of Des Moines. Instead, they swerved and ran east through southern Iowa to the Mississippi River, where they connected with routes in Illinois. Clinton, a frequently used crossing point, reputedly had a cave where fugitive slaves were hidden. There was another river crossing at Burlington, where Starr's Cave (see Section I) was allegedly a hiding place. None of the routes crossed northeastern Iowa, where most of the state's caves are found.

Several houses in Iowa, former "stations" on the Underground Railroad, conduct tours. Among them is the Lewelling Quaker Shrine, (800) 421-4282 (called the "Ticket Office of the Underground Railroad"), in Salem, where you can peer into a crawlspace under the house where runaway slaves were hidden. At the Hitchcock House, (712) 769-2323, in Lewis, you can tour a cellar that was used as a hiding place. The Jordan House, (515) 225-1286, in West Des Moines, contains a museum dedicated to the Underground Railroad in Iowa. The Todd House, (712) 629-2675, in Tabor, also has tours. Although some of these houses originally had tunnels running to other buildings, the tunnels were later filled in or have since collapsed. Nothing remains in Iowa that is comparable to the subterranean tour at the Milton House in Wisconsin. For more information, see the National Park Service Web site at www.cr.nps.gov/nr/travel/underground

Herbert Hoover, 31st president of the United States, was a native of Iowa and a world-famous mining engineer. Courtesy of the Herbert Hoover Presidential Library.

The "Man of the World" exhibit details Hoover's travels as a globe-trotting "doctor of sick mines." He began his own consulting firm, establishing offices around the world. His lectures at the Columbia School of Mines, published in 1909 as *Principles of Mining*, was a standard college textbook for many years. The silver mines of Burma became the basis of his personal fortune, and he was called in to survey the Romanoff mines of Russia. In all he visited 40 nations on four continents and was dubbed "the Great Engineer." For "relaxation" while traveling, he undertook, with the aid of his wife, the English translation of the great mining classic of the Middle Ages, Agricola's *De Re Metallica*, originally published in Latin in 1556.

Stirred by the ordeal of Belgium in World War I, a country cut off from food supplies by the Germans, Hoover formed the Belgian Relief Committee, a controversial move at the time because the Allies feared that any donated food would fall into German hands. Hoover later wrote, "My engineering career was over. I was on the slippery road of public life." He served in President Woodrow Wilson's U.S. Food Administration and, as director of the American Relief Administration, helped feed 350 million people in 21 countries. There are hundreds of tributes to Hoover in the display, "A World of Thanks."

Hoover initiated "Operation Pack Rat" even as World War I raged. Its goal was to salvage documents pertaining to the war. They were eventually housed at the Hoover Institution of War, Revolution, and Peace, which he founded at Stanford.

Hoover served as Secretary of Commerce in the 1920s. When he took office, the secretary was only expected to "put the fish to bed at night and turn out the lights around the coast," but Hoover was a dynamo. He promoted standardization and the elimination of waste in industry. He dealt with new industries such as aviation and radio. During the great Mississippi River flood of 1927 he mobilized the relief operation. He planned Hoover Dam—later renamed Boulder Dam by his political foes.

Hoover's inauguration platform and a display entitled "Living in the White House" (1928–1932) are compelling attractions at the museum, as is a re-creation of his Camp Rapidan cabin in the Shenandoah Mountains. Hoover was often blamed for the Great Depression and for favoring voluntary relief over direct federal handouts. Yet it was later said that many of the ideas enacted during the terms of his successor, Franklin Delano Roosevelt, had originally been thought of by the Hoover administration.

After World War II, Hoover played a role in the development of the Marshall Plan to bring economic and political stability to Europe. He also headed the two Hoover Commissions, which examined waste in the federal government caused by the duplication of activities created by the welter of agencies that had sprung up. The display entitled "The Waldorf Towers, Suite 31-A" is a re-creation of the hotel room where he spent the last years of his life. At the exit, there is another statue of Hoover as angler—echoing the one at the museum's entrance. The nearby Quarton Gallery features temporary exhibits.

The adjacent Herbert Hoover National Historic Site preserves historic properties associated with his life. Basically, the site represents an entire Midwestern farm community, including a restored tallgrass prairie. Go to the visitor center, then walk through the town, which includes the two-room cottage where Hoover was born, the blacksmith shop run by his father, the one-room schoolhouse he attended, the Friends Meetinghouse where he worshipped, and his grave site on the hill.

Directions: The museum is located just off Interstate 80. Take Exit 254 and go north on County Road X30 a short distance.

Season/hours: Daily, 9:00 a.m. to 5:00 p.m., except Christmas, Thanksgiving, and New Year's Day. Fee.

Precautions: None. It's wheelchair accessible.

Amenities: Gift shop. The Herbert Hoover National Historic Site includes a picnic area.

Contact: Herbert Hoover Presidential Library and Museum, Box 488, 210 Parkside Drive, West Branch, IA 52358. Phone: (319) 643-5301 or (319) 643-2541. Web site: www.hoover.nara.gov

Old Brewery Art Gallery and Museum
Clayton County

TWENTY FEET under the town of Guttenberg, a skull grins at you from a gap in the crumbling stone wall of a brewery vault. The Old Brewery building has an interesting history dating back to 1856. It served as the Jungk Brewery from 1875 to 1884 and remained in the Jungk family until 1970. The brewery was then used as a rental property until one day a giant boulder from the towering bluffs behind the building came crashing down through the rear wall. Thereafter, the building remained derelict until it was purchased in 1987 by two artists, Naser and Patricia Shahrivar.

The Shahrivars labored for five years to restore the gutted shell of the brewery. Rumor had it that there were gold coins hidden about the premises, which gave them an additional incentive! They transformed the brewery into an art gallery, studio, residence, and a three-room bed and breakfast. The charming suites are named after the Jungks' daughters, Evelyn, Lucille, and Viola.

Most interesting from a subterranean point of view, however, is the cavernous storage cellar under the brewery. Reached by a steep stairway inside the brewery, the cellar is located 20 feet below the surface. The cellar is a cool 50 degrees Fahrenheit, providing refrigeration

Decide for yourself whether this skull, resting in a chink in the wall of the Old Brewery Cellar in Guttenberg, is real or fake!

for the beer that was stored there. Reportedly, it is one of three such cellars; the other two, at deeper levels, were sealed off at some time in the past for unknown reasons.

The rectangular cellar, constructed of native limestone, is approximately 20 by 30 feet and 10 feet high. There are foot-long, white soda-straw stalactites hanging from the barrel-vaulted stone ceiling as well as reddish, iron-stained stalactites. A collection of other mineral formations found growing in the cellar is displayed on a table. The floor is built up from several layers of red brick. During the Mississippi River flood of 1993, the cellar was awash in a foot of water.

Several years ago the cellar was decorated for Halloween and some of the spooky items were left up, creating an almost dungeonlike atmosphere that kids will love. In the far wall there is a chink in the masonry containing the aforementioned skull. The Shahrivars insist that it's only a replica—but it's hard to say. The cellar has interesting acoustical properties, and the couple says that one of their regular guests goes down there late at night to play musical instruments in the dim, eerie light.

There are stories of other caves on the property as well. In the basement of the now-demolished icehouse, it is believed that there were caves that led back into the bluff. Perhaps they were abandoned lead mines, which are common in Guttenberg. Unfortunately, the icehouse was torn down in 1958, and the basement was filled in with debris, so any other caves are inaccessible.

On the outskirts of Guttenberg, just south of town on U.S. Highway 52, check out the breathtaking overlook of the Mississippi Valley. A sign at the pull-out states that "This particular bluff contains the most complete exposure of the Galena Group rocks known." It goes on to explain caves, sinkholes, and algific slopes.

Directions: From U.S. Highway 52, where it passes through Guttenberg, head west on Goethe Street to where it meets the bluff at Bluff Street. The Old Brewery is located at the T intersection.

Season/hours: Daily, 10:00 a.m. to 6:00 p.m., May through December; 10:00 a.m. to 5:00 p.m., January through April; or by appointment. Free.

Length: 30 feet.

Precautions: Steep flight of stairs leading to the cellar.

Amenities: The Shahrivars operate a bed and breakfast, and guests receive a complimentary glass of wine or a cold mug of beer fresh from the tap. There is also a gallery of art for sale. The Old Brewery is just minutes from downtown Guttenberg.

Contact: Naser and Patricia Shahrivar, 402 South Bluff Street, P.O. Box 217, Guttenberg, IA 52052. Phone: (800) 353-1307 or (563) 252-2094. Web site: www.alpinecom.net/artandbandb

56

Bertrand Museum
Harrison County

W HEN YOU THINK of hunting for sunken treasure-laden ships, you might picture the daring exploits of underwater divers. The remains of the steamboat Bertrand however, were found deep under the Nebraska sod, far from water. The vessel now forms the centerpiece of a museum set in the De Soto National Wildlife Refuge in far western Iowa.

On April 1, 1865, the Bertrand was on its maiden voyage when it struck a snag in the DeSoto Bend of the Missouri River and sank in 12 feet of water. The stern-wheeler was carrying supplies upriver from St. Louis, Missouri, to the Rocky Mountain gold camps. No one drowned, but an estimated one hundred tons of cargo was lost. Valuables such as gold bullion, flasks of mercury (used in refining gold), and the boat's engine were salvaged soon after. The "Big Muddy" rapidly sealed the wreck in clay and silt, protecting it from decay. Of the more than four hundred steamboats that have sunk in the Missouri River, the Bertrand's state of preservation is exceptional. Many steamboats also sank on the Mississippi River, especially in the treacherous rapids along the Iowa stretch, but these were removed during the course of channel dredging by the Army Corps of Engineers.

Over time, the Missouri River shifted its course, leaving the Bertrand almost a mile inland and 30 feet underground. The sunken steamboat, a veritable time capsule, was relocated in 1967 with the use of metal detectors and soil borings. More than two hundred wells were installed around the hull to lower the water table enough for a full-scale excavation to begin. What remained of the boat's cargo, referred to as the "Bertrand Stores," more than 200,000 artifacts, was recovered in the following years. The collection was opened to the public in 1981.

The heart of the Bertrand Museum is the Cargo Gallery, which is labeled, "April 1, 1865: A Moment Frozen in Time." This darkened hall can easily remind you of an exhibit of items recovered from the Titanic. Vast numbers of artifacts, a veritable subterranean Wal-Mart, are visible behind floor-to-ceiling glass in climate-controlled cham-

Like a time capsule buried in the mud, the steamboat Bertrand, which sank in the Missouri River in 1865, is preserved as a priceless treasure. Photo by Cindy Doty.

bers. The Civil War–era Bertrand Stores rival the best period collections in the country. Among the stores are picks and shovels for the gold mines; hammers and saws to build dwellings; cannonballs and powder kegs to defend them; clothing, glassware, and crockery; patent medicines; and preserved foodstuffs. An eight-foot-long scale model of the Bertrand occupies the center of the gallery.

One exhibit describes human impact on the Missouri River basin. It contains displays such as "Striking It Rich," which deals with the 1860s Montana gold rush for which the Bertrand was bringing supplies; "Cutting the Tall Timber;" and "Bustin' the Sod." A video, Seeds of Change, explains the concept in detail. The center also includes treehouse-style enclosures for viewing waterfowl.

After touring the visitor center, don't leave the wildlife refuge without visiting the actual excavation site of the Bertrand, which is on the National Register of Historic Places. Driving to the wreck, about three miles west of the museum, you actually cross over into Nebraska.

A Nebraska historical marker faces the parking lot at the wreck site. Follow a footpath to a green, oval pond in the woods. An observation platform overlooking the pond includes interpretive plaques. The 178-foot hull of the steamboat, which was left to reflood after the cargo was removed (to retard decay), is not visible in the murky water, but it is outlined with white buoys. It takes a bit of imagination to visualize how the Missouri River might have run through this spot.

Follow the Bertrand Trail down to the old river channel, and you will get a feel for what steamboats like the Bertrand had to contend with.

The DeSoto National Wildlife Refuge, more than 8,000 acres in size, is located on the Missouri River Flyway for waterfowl migrating between Arctic nesting grounds and Gulf Coast wintering areas. The refuge is best known for its snow geese.

Directions: From Interstate 29, north of Council Bluffs, take Exit 75 at the town of Missouri Valley. Go west on U.S. Highway 30 for five miles; watch for signs on the left.

Season/hours: The museum is open daily, 9:00 a.m. to 4:30 p.m., except New Year's Day, Easter, Thanksgiving, and Christmas. The excavation site and other recreational facilities are open daily, daylight hours only. Vehicle entry fee.

Precautions: There are warning signs about poison ivy at the excavation site.

Amenities: The De Soto Visitor Center contains a bookstore. Picnic tables are placed along the 12-mile Wildlife Drive that runs through the refuge.

Contact: De Soto National Wildlife Refuge, 1434 316th Lane, Missouri Valley, IA 51555. Phone: (712) 642-2772. Web site: www.recreation.gov

57
Harmon Tunnel
Madison County

WHEN PEOPLE HEAR about a Devil's Backbone Park, they usually think of the state park of that name in northern Iowa. But there's also a state park in southern Iowa that used to have the same name and for a similar reason: a suitably shaped ridge of rock carved by a meandering river. (It's a popular moniker: neighboring Missouri has 25 rock formations named "Devil's Backbones"!) The southern Iowa park was renamed Pammel State Park years ago in honor of Louis H. Pammel, a botanist frequently called the "Father of Iowa State Parks." Pammel's "backbone" harbors some of the oldest oak trees in Iowa, dating to the 1630s.

A bronze plaque affixed to the tunnel that pierces the rocky back-

When visitors tire of the bridges of Madison County, they should try the Harmon Tunnel at nearby Pammel State Park.

The Deepest Hole in Iowa

The deepest hole in the world was drilled on the Kola Peninsula above the Arctic Circle in the former Soviet Union from 1970 to 1984. That hole, nearly 7.5 miles deep, was drilled to examine the Earth's crust and metal-bearing zones at great depths. The deepest hole in Iowa, however, was created in 1987 when the Amoco Production Company, searching for oil, drilled a test well near the town of Halbur in Carroll County to a depth of 17,851 feet—more than three miles.

The location of the Amoco hole was carefully chosen based on the plate tectonic history of Iowa. One billion years ago, the continent of North America nearly split in half. Huge volumes of molten lava poured out onto the surface and solidified. The result, called the Midcontinent Rift, is a geological scar that runs 950 miles from Lake Superior to Kansas. At Duluth, Minnesota, rocks related to the Midcontinent Rift can be seen on the surface, but farther south, where the rift crosses Iowa from northeast to southwest, these same rocks are buried deep within the earth. Since the rocks of the rift are denser and more magnetic than the surrounding rocks, the rift carries a prominent signature that allows geophysicists to map it, despite its depth.

Most oil is found in rocks younger than one billion years old. But in Michigan, there is a copper mine in rift-related rocks, and oil drips from the roof. It was therefore thought that the sediments in the basins flanking Iowa's underground rift might be a good place to look for trapped oil. However, when geologists analyzed samples brought up from the Amoco well, they found that the rocks were "overmature;" that is, they had been too hot in the past—hot enough to destroy any oil that had been there. However, it's still possible that at other places in the rift, oil will someday be found.

bone offers a thumbnail sketch of the park's history: "Where William Harmon and his three sons dug through the soft black shale of the backbone, completing in 1858 the waterway tunnel which provided water power for the old mill; first used as saw mill, later as grist mill— abandoned as mill in 1904; completed as highway tunnel in 1925."

Before the tunnel was built, the Middle River, which flows through the heart of Madison County, had carved a horseshoe bend in the local bedrock, leaving the central ridge as the "backbone" over one hundred feet high. At the ridge's narrowest point, Harmon dug a tunnel six feet high, six feet wide, and one hundred feet long. He then built a brush dam to divert water from the higher level of the river on the west side of the ridge to the lower level on the east side where the mill wheel was located. The tunnel thus by-passed a loop in the river. Floods, however, gnawed away at the soft walls of the tunnel until it became 40 feet wide. Mill tunnels are not uncommon in the Midwest, but the subsequent conversion of this one to be able to carry vehicular traffic makes it unique. Reportedly, it's the only highway tunnel in Iowa.

Today, the white limestone of the backbone is visible above the tunnel entrance, wreathed in foliage. People entering the tunnel, now 15 feet high, 40 feet wide, 100 feet long and lined with concrete, are greeted with a stiff breeze. Automobile traffic passes in both directions, and sidewalks line both sides of the tunnel's interior. Drivers entering the tunnel sometimes give a "courtesy tap" on the horn to warn drivers approaching from the opposite direction.

Directions: From State Highway 92, just west of Winterset, turn south on County Road P68 for three miles and enter Pammel State Park. The highway passes directly through the Harmon Tunnel.

Season/hours: Daily, 4:00 a.m. to 10:30 p.m. Free.

Length: 100 feet.

Precautions: No lights required. Sight lines at both ends of the tunnel are short, and cars abruptly appear out of nowhere. Some drivers honk before entering the tunnel as a warning, others do not. A sign at the entrance to the tunnel warns, "Impassable During High Water."

Amenities: Picnicking, camping, and fishing in Pammel State Park. Winterset, the birthplace of John Wayne, and the famous covered bridges of Madison County, are nearby.

Contact: Madison County Conservation Board, Box 129, Winterset, IA 50273. Phone: (515) 462-3536. Web site: www.madisoncountyparks.org

58

Grotto of the Redemption
Palo Alto County

T HE MIDWESTERN tradition of grotto building began with
Father Paul Dobberstein (1872–1954), at West Bend, Iowa, in
1912. Described as a "petrified mirage" on the prairie, his great
creation, the Grotto of the Redemption, inspired similar efforts such
as the Dickeyville and Rudolph grottoes in Wisconsin and perhaps
even the famous Watts Towers of Los Angeles.

Father Dobberstein—whose name in German means a dauber, or
plasterer, of stones—was born in Germany, where he became fasci-
nated with geology. He emigrated to the United States and entered a
Catholic seminary in Milwaukee. Upon contracting pneumonia, he
made a vow that if he should live, he would erect a shrine to the
Blessed Virgin. He survived and was subsequently appointed pastor of
Saints Peter and Paul Church at West Bend in 1898, a town named
after its location near a sharp, westward bend in the Des Moines River.
But he never forgot his promise to God.

Father Dobberstein stockpiled stones for more than a decade
before actual construction of the grotto began. Local farmers were
only too happy to rid themselves of the glacial boulders that studded
their fields. The priest drew inspiration for his shrine from the natural, mountainside grottoes visited by Alpine shepherds during the
Middle Ages. He dug down 20 feet to a layer of hardpan, which hinted
at the massive edifice he intended to construct—the "Eighth Wonder
of the World."

Because the West Bend area had relatively few rock outcrops to
quarry, Father Dobberstein resorted to a novel building material—
concrete—then being used to build the grain elevators springing up
on the Iowa prairies. He bejeweled the concrete so densely with semi-
precious stones that the utilitarian material was not even visible
underneath. Taking on the mantle of the spelunker-priest, Father
Dobberstein hitched rides on westbound trains, scouring caves in the
Black Hills and filling gunnysacks with crystals to decorate his
expanding shrine, which would eventually grow to nine separate grottoes. Although this was a well-accepted practice at the time, it would
bring condemnation—and prosecution—today. He loved to tell stories about getting lost in caves, seeing a metaphor for human exis-

tence in the experience.

Father Dobberstein was friendly with Jim White, the cowboy, guano miner, and promoter of Carlsbad Caverns in New Mexico, and obtained from him a stalagmite several feet high, with which he crowned one of the grottoes. In the Grotto of the Ten Commandments, the innovative priest chose to grow his own stalactites. He drilled a hole in the roof of the grotto, allowing rainwater to seep through a mass of lime, resulting in the growth of artificial stalactites on the ceiling!

Father Dobberstein used a variety of materials to embellish the concrete surfaces. Brown jasper rock and petrified wood were the most common. Crystals were arranged in rosettes. Since the site was exposed to the elements, he naturally favored insoluble minerals such as quartz and barite. Several forms of quartz were used, such as amethyst and rose. Keokuk geodes, their gaping mouths toothed with sharp quartz crystals, were also employed. He drew upon all the hues of the mineral palette. White was often used to symbolize purity. Copper minerals provided bright blues and greens. He scorned the use of broken colored glass, so common in other grottoes. The geological value of this grotto is currently estimated at over four million dollars.

Dobberstein was indefatigable, sometimes working the whole night through, his fingers raw and bleeding from continual work with cement. Starting from a single grotto—Mary's Grotto, the fulfillment of his vow—the complex grew over the next 42 years to cover a city block, crowned with a massive artificial mountain 40 feet high, honeycombed with cavelike spaces. He adopted the Egyptian pyramid builder's practice of using long ramps and rollers to get heavy slabs up to the top. His successor, Father Louis Greving, who retired in 1996, introduced an electric hoist, speeding up the work considerably.

The Grotto of the Redemption as a whole consists of nine grottoes, illustrating the story of the Redemption (from the Fall of Man to the Resurrection) and the 14 Stations of the Cross. Because of the continually shifting perspectives and multiple levels within the labyrinthine grotto, you do not readily tire of it. Sixty-five white Carrara marble statues, carved by Italian sculptors, embellish the grounds. At night, the great grotto-mountain is illuminated with floodlights.

Some of the grottoes represent actual historical caves. For example, Mary is traditionally said to have given birth to Jesus in a stable, but others describe it as a cave—the Nativity Cave. The Grotto of Bethlehem, representing this cave, was made with 65 tons of petrified wood. Likewise, Jesus was laid in a rock-cut tomb after the Crucifixion—represented here by the Grotto of the Resurrection.

The archway leading to the Stations of the Cross is flanked by

Father Paul Dobberstein, who began constructing the Grotto of the Redemption at West Bend in 1912, sparked a Midwestern tradition of grotto building.

spherical sandstone concretions from the Cannon Ball River in North Dakota, painted to resemble world globes. The river, by the way, was indeed named after these unusual stones.

An unfortunate accident in 1922 first attracted widespread attention to Father Dobberstein's grotto. He built a bear pit to contain live bears—inspired by his memories of the famous bear pits of Berne, Switzerland—but one of the animals injured a little girl. A nasty legal battle ensued, and it put the grotto firmly on the map. Unfazed, Father Dobberstein transformed the bear pit into the foundation of a new grotto.

Underground Gas Storage

Liquefied petroleum gas (LPG) has been stored in caverns excavated in shale in Iowa since the 1960s. Pipelines bring LPG from the western states and it is then pumped into these caverns. Under Des Moines, for example, there are triple-stacked caverns at depths of 375 feet, 595 feet, and 1,410 feet. The huge tractors used to dig the caverns had to be lowered down shafts one piece at a time, reassembled below, then disassembled and hoisted back up when the job was completed.

In contrast, the underground storage of natural gas by pipeline companies does not involve caverns. The gas is injected into large stretches of deep-seated sandstone, such as Saint Peter Sandstone, where it occupies the pores between the grains. These storage sites, about one-half mile below the surface, are at much greater depths than are the LPG caverns.

The natural-gas storage sites, which can hold more than one hundred billion cubic feet of gas, have to meet several criteria. There must be an upward fold in the rock layers—called an anticline—to trap the gas once it is injected. The layer above the sandstone must be impermeable, forming an upper seal. The sandstone must be saturated with groundwater, forming a lower seal. The water maintains the gas under pressure and drives it back out, like a piston, when required.

The advantages of this method of underground gas storage are safety, economics, and operational flexibility. No dangerous or expensive aboveground storage facilities need to be maintained. The reservoir serves as a buffer for a seasonally fluctuating market. For example, if there is low demand for gas, the excess is pumped into the rocks. If there is high demand, gas is released into the pipeline for consumption.

As if tending to a large parish, erecting a parochial school, excavating an artificial lake (Grotto Lake, of course), and building the grotto itself were not enough, the tireless priest accepted commissions for "satellite" grottoes elsewhere in Iowa and in surrounding states. He developed a system of prefabrication, whereby panels of rosettes could be made in his West Bend workshop and shipped to the sites. From the very beginning, he had the help of a devoted layman, Matthew Szerensce, whom he called "my good right arm," and many others, including school children, who could be drafted into the sacred enterprise.

Natural weathering processes, such as the freeze-thaw action of Iowa winters, took a heavy toll on the grotto, requiring constant upkeep. Father Dobberstein accordingly reserved his most precious and delicate minerals for an indoor site, the Christmas Chapel, set within his parish church, which stands next door. The construction of another grotto that he envisioned—the Grotto of Pentecost—is currently under consideration.

The Grotto Welcome Center, containing a museum, is a must-see. It is located across the street from the grotto itself. Here you can view a large collection of rocks, minerals, and fossils, including the Father Verne Stapenhorst Collection. Especially interesting are minerals from Iowa caves and mines. Much historical grotto memorabilia, including the very hand tools used by Father Dobberstein, is on display, and videos tell the story of the grotto.

With about 80,000 visitors a year, the grotto prides itself on being ecumenical and welcomes people of all faiths. Father Dobberstein (affectionately known as "Dobby") is commemorated with a bronze statue next to the grotto. In 2001, the grotto was added to the National Register of Historic Places.

Directions: From Interstate 35, take U.S. Highway 18 west to State Highway 15, go south to West Bend. Turn west onto 4th Street NE and south on Broadway Avenue. The grotto occupies a city block along the west side of Broadway.

Season/hours: Open year round. Guided tours every hour May through October. A freewill donation of $5.00 per adult and $2.50 per child is requested to carry on the work of maintaining the grotto.

Length: Various. Allow at least two hours.

Precautions: In winter, ice creates a slip hazard.

Amenities: Grotto Welcome Center, Grotto Café, Grotto Giftshop. A 100-site campground with electrical hookups is available next to the grotto.

Contact: Grotto of the Redemption, Box 376, West Bend, IA 50597. Phone: (800) 868-3641 or (515) 887-2371. Web site: www.westbendgrotto.com

Appendix
More Iowa
Caving Opportunities

THE FOLLOWING is an annotated list of additional public caving opportunities in the state of Iowa, arranged by county. Compared with the main entries in this guide, these caves are often smaller, and the caying areas afford prospecting opportunities for those who want to try their hand at finding their own caves. If you do go, remember that it is always easier to find caves when there are no leaves on the trees. Respect landowner rights, and wear blaze orange during hunting season.

If you would like to get into caving more seriously after reading this book, I urge you consider joining the Iowa Grotto, the local branch of the National Speleological Society, which can provide specialized training. Founded in 1949, this cave club holds monthly meetings at Trowbridge Hall on the University of Iowa Campus in Iowa City and for many years has published a sterling newsletter, *The Intercom*, which has won several awards. Their address is Iowa Grotto, Box 228, Iowa City, IA 52244.

Boone County

Ledges State Park. It has often been remarked that this park, named for its unusual rock formations, "looks like" it should contain caves. Try your luck!

Cedar County

Massillon Park. The scenic Wapsipinicon River bluffs feature "natural wells" (sinkholes) depicted on old postcards. Located on County Road Y24 in the town of Massillon.

Cerro Gordo County

Interstate Park. There are rumors of caves in the limestone bluffs of the Willow Creek gorge in downtown Mason City.

Lime Creek Nature Center. On U.S. Highway 65 north of Mason City. Hiking the Brewery Loop brings you to the gated cellar of the

Spring Brewery (1873–1882).

Clayton County

Camp Ewalu. This Lutheran bible camp located near Strawberry Point has a cave about 50 feet long, entered through a sinkhole.

Clinton County

Eagle Point City Park. Located in Clinton. Contains rockshelters.

Delaware County

Hardscrabble Park. Hardscrabble Cave is a 15-foot crawling cave in dolomite outcrops along the Maquoketa River. From Hopkinton, drive west on County Road D47, and turn south into the park after crossing the river.

Retz Wildlife Area. Located three miles west of Delhi along gravel roads. Has several small caves.

Dubuque County

Roosevelt Park. Features the Storybook Hill Children's Zoo (open in summer only). Located on Cascade Road southwest of downtown Dubuque. Caves have been reported in the dolomite outcrops along the South Fork of Catfish Creek where it winds through the park.

Fayette County

Gouldsberg Park. On County Road W14, five miles north of Hawkeye, along the Little Turkey River. A mechanical cave with several hundred feet of passages and old graffiti.

Volga River State Recreation Area. If you'd like to combine cave hunting with horseback riding, here's your opportunity! More than thirty miles of trails wind through one of Iowa's best equestrian parks. The lengthy trails—often over featureless ground—are less suitable as hiking trails. Reportedly, there are caves in the limestone outcrops along the Lima Trail, which skirts the Volga River.

Fremont County

Spring Valley Loop, Loess Hills National Scenic Byway. A tourist brochure claims that "Half hidden caves or cellars (many are brick faced) can be seen from the road."

Waubonsie State Park. Near Hamburg. Reportedly contains abandoned loess cellars that were dug by early settlers to store apples and were converted into dwellings during the Great Depression.

Hardin County

Iowa City. Some of the huge overhangs in the scenic Iowa River gorge qualify as rockshelters. Where Preston Street meets the river, you will see a sign for Hawkeye Street. Park your car and walk down the lengthy concrete stairway to the public picnic area below the dam, where you will find several good examples.

Jackson County

Bellevue State Park (Nelson Unit). A mechanical cave about 50 feet long can be found in the sandstone cliffs along the park access road, three-tenths of a mile uphill from the entrance gate. Other caves reportedly exist in the park, which is located just south of Bellevue on Highway 52 along the Mississippi River.

Big Mill Wildlife Area. Several talus (boulder) caves have been found along Big Mill Creek. Located five miles west of Bellevue on County Road D57.

Pine Valley Nature Area. Pine Valley Cave, a large rock shelter, is located in the outcrops along Pine Creek. From the parking lot (located on 30th Avenue, 1.5 miles south of County Road E17 near the town of Emeline), hike the Red & Yellow Trail down into the valley; the cave is located in the first outcrops you come to. Several more caves can be found in the valley by off-trail hiking.

Mills County

Oak Township. There are rumors of several horse-thief caves here!

Van Buren County

Douds Stone, Inc. An operating limestone mine, said to be the largest underground mine in Iowa. More than 80 acres has been mined out. Privately owned and operated, visitors are sometimes allowed to see the operation with permission.

Webster County

Dolliver Memorial State Park. South of Fort Dodge. There are rumors of caves in Boneyard Hollow and along the Copperas Trail.

Winneshiek County

Bear Creek Park. Reportedly contains caves in the Oneota dolomite. On County Road A24 near Highlandville. Also visit nearby Mestad Springs.

Bluffton Fir Stand State Preserve. A rounded, frost-shattered rock shelter known as "The Oven" can be seen high in the bluffs of the Upper Iowa River overlooking the town of Bluffton. Park on the road along the west side of the preserve, hike up the steep trail (very strenuous) that parallels the edge of the bluff, and check out the outcrops when you are aligned with the long, north-south street in the town below. Not recommended for those afraid of heights!

Upper Iowa River. This 135-mile river is indisputably the most scenic "cave river" in the whole state! Rent a canoe and see the many caves and springs along its banks. Canoe rentals are available at Kendallville, Bluffton, and Decorah.

Glossary

of Caving and Mining Terms

accidental—An animal that enters a cave by accident, as by falling through a sinkhole, but does not actually live there.

adit—A horizontal or sloping mine entrance, as distinguished from a shaft (vertical entrance).

aggregate—Sand and gravel.

algific—Literally, "cold producing;" a term applied to north-facing slopes that are cooled in summer by air from hidden ice caves in the underlying bedrock, creating a special microclimate that favors northern plants.

amphipod—A shrimplike crustacean a fraction of an inch long, found in many Iowa springs. Also called a scud, it is a favorite food of trout.

anthodites—A mineral flower composed of radiating clusters of aragonite crystals.

aragonite—A mineral composed, like calcite, of calcium carbonate, but with different crystallization and other characteristics.

backbone—A rock ridge, often the core of a meander loop of a river.

bituminous coal—An intermediate rank of coal, of the kind mined in Iowa, more evolved than lignite but less so than anthracite.

blackjack—Zinc sulfide (sphalerite), an ore found below the water table in zinc mines.

bone—Shale, as found in coal seams.

brachiopod—A bivalved shellfish, also called a lampshell. Pentamerid brachiopods are called "fossil pig's feet" or "devil's claws."

calcite—The most common form of calcium carbonate, the mineral making up limestone and many cave formations.

cave pearls—Pearl-like concretions of calcite, formed in shallow cave pools by dripping water.

chert—A microgranular form of quartz.

chockstone—A stone wedged between the walls of a cave passage, often useful as a foothold.

coralloids—Nodular, coral-like speleothems such as grapes and popcorn.

crinoids—Flowerlike animals, also known as sea lilies, that formed extensive submarine meadows during the Mississippian Period, and are most commonly represented by pieces of their stems, called "Cheerios" fossils.

damp—A dangerous mine gas, such as carbon dioxide (black damp, also called choke damp), carbon monoxide (white damp), or methane (fire damp).

dolomite—A term that refers both to a mineral, calcium magnesium carbonate, and to magnesium-rich limestones.

drift—(1) Glacial deposits; (2) a horizontal mine passage.

dripstone—Speleothems, such as stalactites and stalagmites, formed by dripping water.

drybone—Zinc carbonate (smithsonite), so called because of its color and porous, earthy texture.

erratic—A stone transported from its parent source to another place by glacial action. Also applied to twisted speleothems like helictites.

falling wedge—A longwall mining technique in which the coal seam is undercut and allowed to fall downwards.

float blocks—Large rocks that have separated from cliffs and slid downhill, producing caves, rock cities, or rock towers. Also called slump blocks.

flowstone—A speleothem formed by thin films of flowing water.

"Frozen waterfalls" are the most spectacular form of flowstone.

galena—Lead sulfide, a major ore of lead, often found as shiny metallic cubes.

geode—A spherical bedrock cavity lined with crystals; Iowa's state rock.

grapes—A nodular wall coating of calcite that resembles grapes; see popcorn.

helictites—A delicate, twisted stalactite that seems to defy gravity; the word is derived from helix.

hematite—A form of iron oxide, the principal ore of iron mined in Iowa, often occurring in red, earthy masses.

hibernaculum—Winter hibernation quarters, as for example bat caves.

karst—A landscape formed by the dissolution of soluble bedrock, usually limestone or dolomite, and characterized by underground drainage, with disappearing streams, sinkholes, caves, and springs.

lepidodendron—One of the most important plants of the Coal Age swamps, growing to a height of more than 100 feet. They are commonly referred to as "coal palm trees" in Iowa, and their fossils are often mistaken for petrified snakeskin because of their pattern of leaf scars.

Liesegang bands—Swirls of reddish iron pigment found in the Saint Peter Sandstone.

loess—A widely distributed wind-deposited soil originating as rock flour, produced by glaciers grinding bedrock during the Ice Ages. Washed out from under the glaciers by streams of melt water, the silt dried and was swept aloft by wind. Iowa's state soil, the Tama, is a loess. Usually pronounced "luss."

longwall mining—A mining method in which a coal seam is excavated along a wide swath, with the mined-out space being supported by timbers and waste material rather than pillars of unmined coal.

mechanical cave—A cave created by earth movements, as when

rocks separate along joints, leaving narrow gaps; the Decorah Ice Cave is an example.

molefoot—A type of drill bit used in coal mining, so called from its appearance; also called moletooth.

mucking—The loading of mine cars with coal or ore.

Niagara Escarpment—A buried reef from the Silurian Period that loops around the Great Lakes, passing diagonally through northeastern Iowa, where it typically manifests itself as a wooded slope. Many of Iowa's most scenic parks are found along this feature. It was named for rock exposures at Niagara Falls.

ore—An economically valuable metallic deposit.

Paleozoic Plateau—Name for what, prior to 1976, had been called the Driftless Area of northeast Iowa, in recognition that some drift is, in fact, found there.

petroglyph—A prehistoric rock carving.

phreatic—Literally, "water-filled;" a term applied to caves formed below the water table.

piping caves—Caves formed by flowing groundwater washing away individual grains of soil or rock.

placer—A mineral deposit, such as gold, in loose sand and gravel.

popcorn—A nodular wall coating of calcite that resembles popcorn; see grapes.

pseudokarst—Landforms that mimic karst but were not created by chemical solution.

rimstone dams—Naturally formed dams that obstruct cave streams.

rock city—Place where giant blocks of rock have separated from the parent cliff just enough to leave intersecting "streets" and "avenues" in the spaces between; also called a "bear town."

rockshelter—A cliff overhang or shallow cave.

room and pillar mining—A mining method in which rooms are

excavated, leaving pillars of unmined material for support.

Scotch hearth—A lead-smelting blast furnace introduced about 1835 that produced lead "pigs" (ingots) weighing about 72 pounds each.

shotcrete—Sprayed concrete, often used in creating imitation caves.

soda straw—Tubular stalactites, about the diameter of a drop of water. Once the tube gets plugged with mineral deposits and water flows on the outside, a typical carrot-shaped stalactite develops.

solution caves—Caves formed by the chemical dissolution of rocks, such as limestone or dolomite, by natural acids, such as carbonic acid.

speleothem—A general term for cave formations.

sphalerite—Zinc sulfide.

springtail—A wingless insect about the size of a sesame seed, often found in caves. The name stems from an abdominal appendage that allows them to spring into the air.

SRT—Abbreviation for "single rope technique," used to explore vertical caves. SRT is a great advance upon the use of bulky rope ladders.

sump—Place where a cave passage is filled to the ceiling with water.

talus caves—Caves formed by the spaces between boulders at the foot of a cliff.

tipple—A surface structure where mine cars are emptied by being tipped.

troglobites—The original meaning of the term was broadly applied to cave-adapted animals, such as blind cave fish, that could not live outside of caves. Some people now restrict the term to the terrestrial forms and distinguish the aquatic forms as stygobites.

troglophiles—Animals, such as many spiders, that prefer caves but are not specially cave adapted.

trogloxenes—Animals, such as bats, that use caves for daily or seasonal shelter but do not reproduce or seek food there.

tufa—A form of porous limestone deposited by springs.

vadose—A term that describes caves above the water table.

vugs—Small Swiss-cheese-like holes in rocks or cave walls, formed by weathering or dissolution by groundwater.

List of Resources

A great number of resources were consulted in the preparation of this book—far too many to list here. I found the following especially helpful.

Books

Alex, Lynn M. *Iowa's Archaeological Past*. Iowa City: University of Iowa Press, 2000.

Anderson, Duane. *Eastern Iowa Prehistory*. Ames: Iowa State University Press, 1981.

———. *Western Iowa Prehistory*. Ames: Iowa State University Press, 1975.

Anderson, Wayne I. *Iowa's Geological Past: Three Billion Years of Change*. Iowa City: University of Iowa Press, 1998.

Federal Writers' Project. *Iowa: A Guide to the Hawkeye State*. Ames: Iowa State University Press, 1986.

Garvin, Paul. *Iowa's Minerals*. Iowa City: University of Iowa Press, 1998.

Geological Society of Iowa. Numerous guidebooks.

Hake, Herbert V. *Iowa Inside Out*. Ames: Iowa State University Press, 1987.

Hedges, James, ed. *Field Trip Guidebook: National Speleological Society Convention*, Decorah: Privately printed, 1974.

Henry, Thomas. *A Guide to Maquoketa Caves State Park*. Des Moines: Iowa Department of Natural Resources, 1993.

Herzog, Ruth, and John A. Pearson. *Guide to Iowa's State Preserves*. Iowa City: University of Iowa Press, 2001.

Hill, Carol, and Paolo Forti. *Cave Minerals of the World*. 2nd ed. Huntsville: National Speleological Society, 1997.

Iowa Grotto of the National Speleological Society. *Iowa Cave Index.* 6th ed. Iowa City: Iowa Grotto of the National Speleological Society, 1959.

Keyes, Charles. *History of Geographic Development in Iowa.* Des Moines: Iowa Geological Survey, 1913.

Knudson, George E. *Decorah Trails and Trolls.* Decorah: Luther College Press, 1976.

———. *A Guide to the Upper Iowa River.* Decorah: Luther College Press, 1971.

———. *Self Guiding Tour of Decorah for Motorists and Cyclists.* Decorah: Luther College Press, 1971.

Mutel, Cornelia F. *Fragile Giants: A Natural History of the Loess Hills.* Iowa City: University of Iowa Press, 1989.

Olin, Hubert. *Coal Mining in Iowa.* Des Moines: The State Mining Board, 1965.

Owen, David Dale. *Report of a Geological Survey of Wisconsin, Iowa, and Minnesota.* Philadelphia: Lippincott, Grambo and Company, 1852.

Park, John R. *A Guidebook to Mining in America.* Miami: Stone Rose Publishing Company, 2000.

Pratt, LeRoy G. *Discovering Historic Iowa.* Des Moines: Iowa Department of Public Instruction, 1975.

Prior, Jean Cutler. *A Regional Guide to Iowa Landforms.* Iowa City: Iowa Geological Survey, 1976.

Schwieder, Dorothy. *Black Diamonds.* Ames: Iowa State University Press, 1983.

Stone, Lisa, and Jim Zanzi. *Sacred Spaces and Other Places: A Guide to Grottos and Sculptural Environments in the Upper Midwest.* Chicago: The School of the Art Institute of Chicago Press, 1993.

Wolf, Robert Charles. *Iowa's State Parks.* Ames: Iowa State University Press, 1991.

Periodicals
Annals of Iowa

Goldfinch

Intercom

Iowa Geology

Iowa Journal of History and Politics

The Iowan

Journal of the Iowa Archeological Society

Palimpsest

Proceedings of the Iowa Academy of Science (continued as the Journal of the Iowa Academy of Science)

Web Sites
www.state.ia.us/parks—The official Web site of the Iowa Department of Natural Resources, providing information on all state parks and preserves. Indispensable!

www.caves.org—The national Speleological Society

www.ecity.net/iaccb—Contact information for all of Iowa's County Conservation Boards (CCBs) and links to those having Web sites. Valuable for researching county parks.

www.igsb.uiowa.edu—The Iowa Geological Survey Bureau.

www.iowacounties.com—"The Complete Guide to Iowa Web Sites"

www.silosandsmokestacks.org—Web site of the Silos and Smokestacks National Heritage Area, a 37-county region in northeastern Iowa "Where the Story of American Agriculture Comes to Life." Includes information about industrial archeology.

www.traveliowa.com—The Iowa Tourism Office Web site. The place to find attractions, accommodations, events, publications, and more.

Index

W